Poison dart frogs like this one eat beetles, ants, and centipedes, among other insects. They need to eat a variety of bugs so their bodies can create the toxins that make them poisonous.

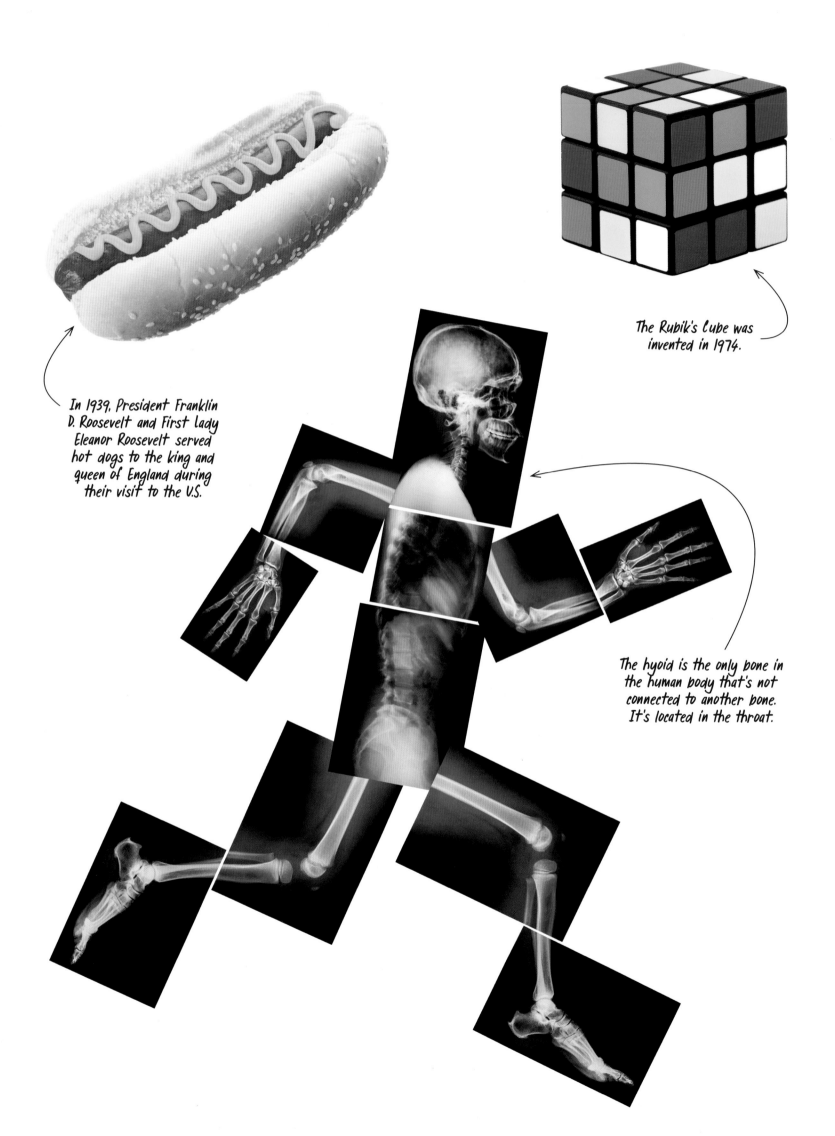

The Rubik's Cube was invented in 1974.

In 1939, President Franklin D. Roosevelt and First Lady Eleanor Roosevelt served hot dogs to the king and queen of England during their visit to the U.S.

The hyoid is the only bone in the human body that's not connected to another bone. It's located in the throat.

TOTALLY RANDOM FACTS vol.1

3,128 Wild, Wacky, and Wondrous Things About the World

Melina Gerosa Bellows

BRIGHT MATTER BOOKS

NEW YORK

Contents

The whiskers around a horse's mouth, nose, and eyes help it sense its surroundings.

Snowflakes aren't white; they're actually translucent.

Tulips are native to Central Asia.

5

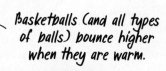

Basketballs (and all types of balls) bounce higher when they are warm.

NASA's Buoyant Rover for Under-Ice Exploration rover (BRUIE) is being developed to one day explore under-ice oceans on other moons and planets in our solar system.

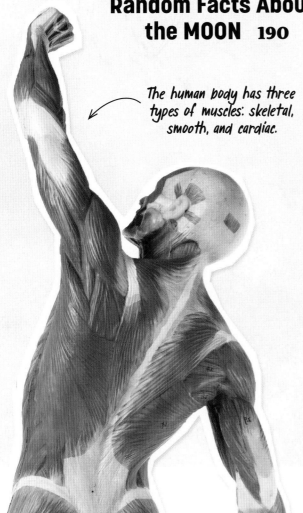

The human body has three types of muscles: skeletal, smooth, and cardiac.

White seeds in a watermelon are seeds that didn't mature.

7

1,476 Totally Random Facts About

Awesome Animals

Flyers, Swoopers, Crawlers, and Chompers

Tooth and Claw

cougar

69 Totally Random Facts About WILDCATS

Most of the 38 cat species are relatively small, but some are considered "big cats"—including the lion, tiger, leopard, jaguar, and snow leopard.

Most big cats are members of the genus *Panthera*.

Cheetahs do not have fully retractable claws.

You can hear an adult lion's roar from up to five miles (8 km) away.

No two tigers have the same patterns of stripes.

The fastest land animal is the cheetah, which can run over 60 miles an hour (96 kmh).

Snow leopards can leap as far as 50 feet (15 m)—which is more than three cars end to end.

Clouded leopards can hang upside down from tree branches.

Jaguars have the strongest jaw muscles of all big cats.

Leopards can drag prey that weighs more than 100 pounds (45 kg)—including antelopes and gazelles—up into trees to prevent hyenas and other animals from stealing it.

The rusty-spotted cat is the smallest wildcat in the world. Fully grown, they weigh about three pounds (1.3 kg).

In general, smaller cats purr but can't roar; big cats roar but can't purr.

Lions live in groups called prides. They are the only big cats that live together.

Female lions—called lionesses—hunt together, bringing down large prey like wildebeests and zebras.

The cougar's range spans from the southern tip of South America up to northwest Canada.

To minimize noise as they run, bobcats step their back feet into the same spots where their front feet have already stepped.

Each of a caracal's ears have more than 20 muscles inside, which help them swivel to detect sounds.

Sand cats live in the deserts of Africa and Asia, where the thick pads on their feet help them walk on slippery desert sands.

Jaguarundis use at least 13 different calls to communicate, including purring, whistling, and chirping.

Margays, adapted for life in the trees, can hang from a branch by just one foot.

THE SIBERIAN TIGER IS THE WORLD'S LARGEST BIG CAT. IT CAN WEIGH UP TO 660 POUNDS (300 KG) AND BE MORE THAN 10 FEET (3 M) LONG.

Jaguars and cheetahs have circular markings called rosettes. You can tell the difference by looking at the center of the markings: Jaguars have spots in the middle of their rosettes, cheetahs don't.

Snow leopards live in mountainous areas of Asia, where they are experts at navigating the steep rocky landscape.

Margays can rotate their hind legs 180 degrees to run headfirst down a tree.

The jaguar is the largest wildcat in the Western Hemisphere.

Jaguars live in 18 countries in Central and South America. Most are found in Brazil.

The fluffy fur of the Pallas's cat—the longest and densest of any cat—changes from brownish yellow and striped in the summer to more of a solid gray in the winter.

A snow leopard's tail is almost as long as its body.

Snow leopards can't roar.

Leopards have the largest range of all of the big cats, spanning roughly 62 countries across much of Africa, Europe, and Asia.

A tiger's stripes help the cat blend in with jungle plants while it hunts for prey.

Servals sometimes go to the water for food, where they can catch up to 30 frogs in three hours.

No photos existed of the Chinese mountain cat in the wild until 2007.

Tigers have teeth that are about the length of a ice pop stick.

Servals rely on their big ears to help them hear their prey's movement when they hunt.

White tigers are very rare. Their coloring is caused by a special gene.

Tigers have spots on the back of their ears that look like eyes.

Some big cats leave their scent in certain places to let other animals know they were there.

Servals are medium-size cats that live on the African savanna. Their extra-long necks help them see over the savanna's tall grasses.

Ancient Egyptians trained cheetahs for hunting.

The cougar goes by many other names, including mountain lion, puma, and panther.

Cheetah

Each individual Amur leopard has a unique pattern of spots.

An Amur leopard's fur grows longer in the winter to help keep it warm.

With just over 80 cats left in the wild, the Amur leopard is one of the most endangered species in the world.

lioness and her cubs

THOUGH THEY ARE NICKNAMED "KING OF THE JUNGLE," LIONS ACTUALLY ONLY LIVE ON GRASSLANDS AND PLAINS.

Big cats tend to respond to catnip in much the same way as house cats.

Cheetahs can bound over 20 feet (6 m) in a single stride.

A "black panther" in the wild is a leopard or jaguar with a special gene that produces a rare dark coat.

Tigers can live for up to 20 years in the wild.

Cheetahs may descend from a small group of the cats that survived the last ice age.

Sometimes dogs are placed with cheetahs in captivity to help keep them calm.

A male tiger in India adopted a litter of orphaned cubs, taking on the role of "mother."

Fishing cats are excellent swimmers that have webbed toes to help them move in the water and a rounded head to help them dive.

Scientists think the tufts on the tips of a lynx's ears might help them hear better.

A lion can run at speeds of up to 50 miles an hour (80 kmh) in short bursts.

How can you tell the age of a male lion? Look at his mane. The darker the mane, the older the lion.

Lions tiptoe to stay quiet—they walk on their padded toes so their heels don't touch the ground.

Lions rest or sleep for up to 20 hours a day.

Tigers rely mostly on sight and sound to locate their prey.

Jaguars eat turtles and have a bite strong enough to pierce a turtle's shell.

Female tigers give birth to an average of two to four cubs every two years.

Mother tigers care for their cubs for two to three years before the youngsters go out on their own.

Tigers hunt and take down large animals to eat, such as deer, pigs, water buffalo, and antelope.

Jaguars live in both tropical rain forests and along the banks of rivers.

A snow leopard's spotted coat helps it blend in with its rocky mountain habitat.

Using its powerful hind legs, a snow leopard can leap six times the length of its body.

Snow leopards use their tails for balance and as a blanket to keep warm in the cold.

Jaguar moms usually have two babies at a time.

Tigers can eat more than 80 pounds (36 kg) of meat in one meal.

THAT'S SO RANDOM:

Tigers Love to Swim!

GIVING YOUR CAT A BATH WILL PROBABLY MAKE IT PRETTY GRUMPY. Aside from a few breeds, such the Maine coon and Abyssinian, **most cats do not like getting their coats wet.** According to wildlife biologists, house cats evolved from desert-dwelling wildcats that lived in dry regions, never having to adapt to life around water. Many big cats, however, are different. **Tigers, leopards, jaguars, and lions that live in the jungle or on the plains have a different relationship with water.** These big cats can often be found lounging near watering holes and lakes. Since they usually hunt at night, these big cats get in the water to stay cool under the day's hot sun. **They even teach their cubs to play in water.** The largest member of the big cat family—the tiger—is an especially stellar swimmer, thanks to its padded paws and muscular build. **Some tigers have crossed rivers 18 miles (29 km) wide.** In addition to cooling off and moving around, tigers use their aquatic abilities to help them hunt, cleverly chasing prey into the water to trap it. Wildlife biologists have even seen tigers swim for fun!

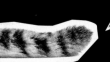
Snow leopard

EACH ONE OF A
TARSIER'S EYES IS
AS BIG AS ITS BRAIN.

All About Primates

Baby bonobo

Monkeys, apes, and lemurs are primates. All primates, including humans, are also mammals. • **Most scientists estimate that there are hundreds of species and subspecies of primates.** • Humans are the only primates that communicate through spoken language, though scientists are working to prove that some other primates may have the ability for speech. • **Almost all primates have hands with five fingers and flat fingernails, not claws.** • Lorises can't jump. • **There are two suborders of primates: Strepsirrhini and Haplorrhini. Strepsirrhini includes lemurs, lorises, and aye-ayes. Haplorrhini includes apes, monkeys, and tarsiers.** • Monkeys that live in Asia and Africa are called Old World monkeys. • **A bush baby's large ears rotate to help it detect insects in the dark.** • Old World monkeys can have snout-like or flat noses • **Marmosets almost always give birth to twins. Dad carries the twins on his back.** • In groups of most Old World monkeys, a female leads the troop. • **Baboons, mandrills, and macaques are all Old World monkeys.** • Lemurs live only in Madagascar and the Comoro Islands, off the coast of Africa. • **Old World monkeys are the largest family of primates.** • Bonobos weren't considered a species until 1929. Before that, they were called "pygmy chimpanzees." • **The male mandrill is the largest Old World monkey, around 35 inches (89 cm) long and weighing 70 to 119 pounds (32–54 kg).** • Most Old World monkeys have tails, but they can't use them to grasp things. • **Monkeys that live in Central and South America are New World monkeys.** • There are more than 150 species of New World monkeys, divided into five families. • **All New World monkeys have flat noses with nostrils that face out.** • The Diana monkey got its name from the Roman goddess of hunting. The lines on the monkey's face look like a hunter's bow. •

MATURE MALE GORILLAS ARE CALLED SILVERBACKS FOR THE SILVERY HAIR THAT GROWS ON THEIR BACK.

Male gorilla

Orangutans rarely come down from trees. • Some New World monkeys have prehensile tails. They can use their tails like an extra hand to grasp things. • **The pygmy marmoset is the world's smallest monkey. It weighs about the same as a bottle of school glue!** • Bush babies are incredible jumpers. They can jump 10 to 16 feet (3–5 m) straight up in one leap as they move through the forest. • **Apes fall into two groups: great apes and lesser apes.** • Gorillas, bonobos, chimpanzees, orangutans, and humans are all great apes. • **Gibbons produce vocalizations known as songs. Females and males will often vocalize, or sing, together, resulting in a duet.** • Humans, chimpanzees, and bonobos have 98 percent of the same DNA. • **Sakis, found in the forests of northern South America, can leap up to 30 feet (9 m) from branch to branch, earning them the nickname "flying**

Young gibbon

Spider monkey

The **SPIDER MONKEY** uses its tail to pick up items as small as a grape.

monkeys." • Howler monkeys are one of the loudest animals in the world. Their sound can be heard from up to 3 miles (4.8 km) away. • **To protect themselves from the rain, orangutans make ponchos and umbrellas out of large leaves.** • Scientists have found that baboons are able to make some vowel-like sounds, which could help experts figure out how human language developed. • **At 460 pounds (209 kg), the eastern lowland gorilla is the largest living primate.** • At only 1.2 ounces (34 g), the smallest living primate is the Madame Berthe's mouse lemur. • **Chimpanzees, gorillas, and orangutans can catch some of the same colds humans get, but for the wild animals, human colds can be very dangerous.** • Slender lorises are nicknamed "bananas on stilts." • **Large groups of gorillas are called troops.** • At 110 to 200 pounds (50–91 kg), the orangutan is the largest fruit-eating animal in the world. • **Vervet monkeys spend several hours grooming one another every day. The most dominant vervets get groomed the most.** • Female gorillas grow to only half the size of male gorillas. • **Apes build nests made out of leaves.** • To check out what's behind and around them, tarsiers can turn their heads nearly 180 degrees in either direction. • **Baboons live in large troops with up to 200 members.** • When moving from place to place, female and young bonobos travel in the middle of the group to stay protected. The dominant male baboons

Male mandrill

stay up front, and less dominant males are in the back. • **Gibbons and siamangs are considered lesser apes. They are smaller than great apes and not as intelligent.** • Lemurs get their name from *lemures*, the Latin word for "evil spirits." • **Chimpanzees live in rain forests, woodlands, and grasslands from central to western Africa.** • Lemurs communicate with others using their scent. Some lemurs flick their scent at each other with their tails. • **Male gorillas beat their chests to communicate their size and strength to prevent other males in the area from challenging them.** • Male gorillas "bluff charge"—they run fast toward another animal to scare it away. • **Wild gorillas are shy and live in dense vegetation.** • The name *marmoset* comes from the French word for dwarf. • **Orangutans are the only great apes that live mostly alone. Gorillas, chimpanzees, and bonobos all live in groups.** • Chimps use medicinal plants to heal themselves. • **Thanks to studying chimps, scientists have identified a plant that could**

Female chimpanzee with her baby

help cure cancer. • Patas monkeys are the fastest runners of all primates. • **New World monkeys have a hairless patch on the tip of their tails. The patches have ridges like fingerprints to help them grip.** • Apes rely more on vision than smell; monkeys depend more on smell. • **Relative to their body size, apes have larger brains than other primates.** • Primates have a bigger brain-to-body-size ratio than other mammals. • **Primates have opposable thumbs.** • Scientists date the first primates back to the Mesozoic era. • **Most primates are social animals that live in groups.** • Compared to other mammals, primates grow slowly. • **Most primates are omnivores, meaning they eat both plants and animals.** • Tarsiers are the only primates that are exclusively meat-eaters. • **Some lemurs are vegetarian, eating only plants.** • In 2020, scientists discovered a new species of monkey in the forests of Myanmar. The Popa langur was named after Mount Popa, an extinct volcano in the area, and is an endangered species. • **About 4 to 7 million years ago in Africa, humans, chimps, and bonobos shared a common ancestor.** • Adult male orangutans grow pads on their cheeks called flanges, which help them attract mates. • **An ape's arms are longer than**

Female orangutan with her baby

ORANGUTAN mothers teach their young how to find food and protect themselves.

SCIENTISTS HAVE SEEN MONKEYS TEACH THEIR YOUNG HOW TO FLOSS THEIR TEETH.

its legs. • Female chimpanzees have babies every five to seven years. • **They make new nests each night.** • Apes can live for 50 years. • **By inflating a pouch in their throats, adult male orangutans can make a loud noise that can be heard a mile (1.6 km) away.** • The siamang monkey, a type of gibbon, has a large throat sac that it inflates when making calls to communicate. • **Apes and humans share blood types.** • The dominant male gorilla settles fights and decides when and where the troop travels. • **Gorillas grunt, screech, and belch.** • Marmosets are the smallest of all monkeys. • **The main diet for gorillas consists of fruit and plants.** • The talapoin monkey lives in the swampy forests of central Africa. At about 14 inches (36 cm) long and only about 2 pounds (0.9 kg), it's one of the smallest

monkeys in the world. • **Adult male gorillas eat up to 45 pounds (20 kg) of food per day.** • Female gorillas can start having babies at 10 years old. • **When inflated, a siamang's throat sac can be as large as a grapefruit.** • Great apes usually have just one baby at a time. • **Baby gorillas start walking when they are 3 to 6 months old; humans start around 8 to 18 months.** • There are two species of gorillas. They both live in Africa. • **Scientists consider chimpanzees to be some of the most intelligent animals on Earth.** • Great apes use sticks as tools to get food and protect themselves. • **Chimpanzees can learn how to play computer games.** • Chimpanzees pant, bark, and hoot. • **Female chimpanzees join a new group when they mature.** • Chimpanzees are omnivores. They eat fruits, plants, seeds, insects, eggs, and even small monkeys. • **Most primates groom one another to show friendship. Chimpanzees comb each other's hair and pull out dirt and bugs.** • Chimps chew up a clump of leaves or use moss to make sponges for drinking water. • **Scientists think that an uakari's pink face might give clues about its**

Slender loris

Talapoin

Ring-tailed lemur

Big Talker!

IN THEIR NATIVE HABITATS, PRIMATES SUCH AS APES AND MONKEYS HAVE MANY FORMS OF COMMUNICATION, including body language, facial expressions, and sounds. But a primate named **Koko, a western lowland gorilla who lived in captivity in California, U.S.A., actually learned a form of sign language.** Over Koko's lifetime, her caregiver taught her to communicate with a vocabulary of more than 1,000 signed words. Koko also understood more than 2,000 words in spoken English. According to experts, Koko the gorilla could communicate as well as a three-year-old human child. **She understood nouns, verbs, and adjectives, and she was able to ask simple questions**—she even asked to have a cat as a pet. When Koko received a lifelike stuffed animal for Christmas instead of a living cat, she was clearly disappointed with the gift. **She signed the word *sad* and refused to play with her new toy.** The next year on her birthday, Koko's wish was finally granted when she was invited to choose a kitten from an abandoned litter. She chose a gray male kitten and named him All Ball. Koko nurtured All Ball and even tried to nurse him. Koko lived to be 46 years old.

health. • Chimpanzee mothers carry their babies on their backs. • **When gibbons walk on tree branches, they usually do so on two feet and sometimes put their hands out for balance.** • Orangutans live only on two islands in Southeast Asia: Sumatra and Borneo. • **Besides humans, the primates that live with their mothers the longest are orangutans—until they are 10 to 12 years old.** • Gorillas walk by pushing off their knuckles. • **An adult male orangutan's arms can stretch some 7 feet (2 m) wide, which is taller than most humans.** • There are three species of orangutans. The newest, the Tapanuli orangutan, was discovered in 2017. • **An orangutan's flexible ankle and knees joints give this ape good balance and allow it to easily grip, jump, and twist as it swings on tree branches.** • One of an orangutan's favorite foods is the fruit of the durian tree. It smells like garlic-flavored cheese. • **The word *orangutan* comes from the Malay term for "person of the forest."** • Orangutans use tree branches to scratch their backs and swat at flies. • **Young apes watch others and learn before trying something new on their own.** • Cotton-top tamarins are named for their fluffy heads of white hair. • **Most great apes are black in color, but orangutans have long, dark red fur.** • The orangutan's predators include tigers, clouded leopards, crocodiles, pythons, wild dogs, and humans. • **Male chimpanzees stay in one group their whole lives.** • Slow lorises have two tongues: one to drink nectar and one to clean its teeth.

ORANGUTANS WERE OBSERVED WATCHING PEOPLE UNTIE A BOAT FROM A DOCK TO RIDE IN. LATER, THEY UNTIED THE BOAT AND WENT FOR A RIDE THEMSELVES.

Red-ruffed lemur

MOST HUMMINGBIRDS BEAT THEIR WINGS BETWEEN 60 AND 80 TIMES A SECOND.

Female ruby-throated hummingbird

Life in the Fast Lane

Bee hummingbird, life-size

30 Totally Random Facts About HUMMINGBIRDS

There are more than 300 species of hummingbirds across North and South America. • **Ecuador has 130 species of hummingbirds, more than any other country in the world.** • Between dawn and dusk, the ruby-throated hummingbird drinks up to half its body weight in nectar. • **Hummingbirds can remember where they ate years later and even which flowers they drank nectar from.** • The ruby-throated hummingbird visits up to 1,000 flowers in one day. • **Hummingbirds have the highest metabolism of all animals when in flight, with the exception of insects.** • Found only in Cuba, the smallest bird in the world is the bee hummingbird. It's about 2 inches (5 cm) long and weighs less than a dime (1.6 g). • **At 8 inches (20 cm) long, the giant hummingbird is the largest hummingbird species on Earth.** • New species of hummingbirds are still being discovered. The blue-throated hillstar was discovered in 2017. • **Hummingbirds pollinate thousands of different plants.** • The heart of the blue-throated mountain-gem beats as fast as 1,260 times a minute. • **Most hummingbirds' hearts beat about 1,200 times a minute. A human's average heart rate is 60 to 100 beats a minute.** • When it's cold, some hummingbirds can reduce their heart rates to as few as 50 beats a minute to save energy. • **The name "hummingbird" comes from the humming sound the birds' wings make as they fly.** • Hummingbirds have flexible shoulder joints that allow their wings to rotate 180 degrees. • **Male Costa's hummingbirds fly in a U-shaped pattern when they dive down in the air.** • Hummingbirds have tiny feet, which reduces drag when they are in flight. • **The Calliope hummingbird is the smallest long-distance migratory bird in the world, traveling more than 5,000 miles (8,000 km) each year.** • In less than one day, the ruby-throated hummingbird has been known to make a nonstop, 500-mile (800 km) flight across the Gulf of Mexico. • **Hummingbirds are the only type of bird that can fly backward for an extended length of time.** • Fossil records show that hummingbirds lived in Europe 30 million years ago. • **Hummingbirds have no sense of smell.** • Hummingbirds can't walk. They can only perch or scoot sideways. • **Female hummingbirds typically lay just two eggs at a time.** • Hummingbird nests are smaller than a half-dollar, and a hummingbird's eggs are sometimes jellybean-size or smaller. • **Some species of hummingbirds make their nests with spider silk and other natural fibers that can stretch to hold the babies as they grow.** • When hummingbirds drink nectar, they move their tongues in and out about 13 times a second. • **A group of hummingbirds can be called a charm, a bouquet, a glittering, a hover, a shimmer, or a tune.** • Hummingbirds can fly 30 miles an hour (48 kmh).

Deep-Sea

Sea turtles are found in tropical and subtropical oceans all over the world.

With the exception of the Arctic and Antarctic, six of the seven species turtles live in nearly every ocean worldwide.

As the largest sea turtle species, leatherbacks top the scales at anywhere from 500 to 2,000 pounds (227–907 kg).

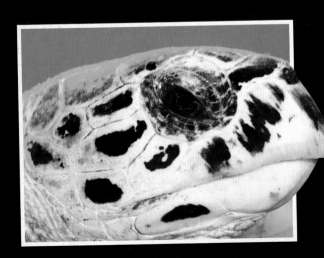

Sea turtles rarely come on land. Females will come to shore to lay their eggs.

Olive ridley sea turtles are named for their pale green, or olive-colored, shells.

Female sea turtles come ashore to lay eggs every two to five years.

Sea turtles have been on Earth for more than 100 million years.

The Kemp's ridley is the smallest species of sea turtle, weighing between 80 and 100 pounds (36–45 kg).

The green sea turtle gets its name from the color of its fat, not the color of its shell.

SEA TURTLES CAN'T PULL THEIR HEAD OR LIMBS INSIDE THEIR SHELLS.

Over their lifetime, female sea turtles can lay thousands of eggs.

After 60 days, sea turtle hatchlings crack out of their shells and head straight for the water.

Sea turtles can hold their breath for four to seven hours while underwater.

Habitat loss, entanglement in fishing nets, and being hunted for food all threaten sea turtles with extinction.

Whether a sea turtle is born male or female depends on the temperature in the nest.

Divers

SEA TURTLES WERE ON EARTH AT THE SAME TIME AS DINOSAURS.

Hatchlings are male if the eggs are incubated below 81.86°F (27.7°C).

Female hatchlings emerge if eggs are incubated above 81.86°F (27.7°C).

Every year, leatherbacks and loggerheads migrate thousands of miles.

Leatherbacks can dive deeper than 4,000 feet (1,219 m), which is the deepest dive of all sea turtle species.

Green sea turtles are the second largest species. They weigh up to 500 pounds (227 kg) and grow up to 4 feet (1.2 m) long.

The shell of a hawksbill sea turtle can be a mix of amber, orange, red, yellow, black, and brown.

All seven species of sea turtles are considered either threatened or endangered.

Sea sponges are a hawksbill's preferred food.

Saltwater crocodiles are a flatback sea turtle's most threatening predator.

The only animals that can dive deeper than leatherbacks are sperm whales, beaked whales, and elephant seals.

The largest leatherback on record was 9 feet (2.7 m) long and estimated to be about 100 years old.

Female hawksbills nest three to five times in one nesting season, which is from April to November. In this time, they lay 130 to 160 eggs.

The loggerhead turtle is named for its large, blocklike head and strong jaws.

Green sea turtles are the only species that visit land to bask in the sun.

Kemp's ridley and olive ridley sea turtles are closely related.

The longest leatherback migration ever tracked was more than 12,000 miles (19,300 km), from the waters of Indonesia to the coast of Oregon in the United States.

Thanks to conservation efforts, Kemp's ridley sea turtles are coming back from the brink of extinction.

The hawksbill sea turtle is named for its narrow head and sharp, birdlike beak, which helps it find food in the crevices of coral reefs.

Flatback turtles are named after their shell, which isn't curved like the shells of other sea turtles.

Sea turtles don't have feet; they have flippers.

Leatherbacks can grow up to 8 feet (2.4 m) long.

Though olive ridley sea turtles usually nest alone, females sometimes come together to nest in large groups.

Warmer temperatures due to climate change are resulting in more female sea turtles being born.

Unlike other sea turtle species, leatherbacks do not possess a hard shell. Instead, they have a tough skin.

Most female sea turtles come ashore to lay eggs on the same beach where they were born.

Sea turtles don't have teeth.

Sea turtles do not have visible ears but do have eardrums covered by skin.

Female flatbacks lay only 50 eggs per batch. Other turtles lay between 100 and 200 eggs.

Sea turtles have light spongelike bones, which help them float.

Male sea turtles spend the vast majority of their lives at sea, rarely ever returning to land after hatching.

Each species of sea turtles eats, rests, and swims in different types of environments.

The bony plates that make up a turtle's shell are called scutes.

When a female turtle is nesting, she appears to shed tears. But she is actually releasing salt that her body doesn't need.

Ninety percent of sea turtle nesting in the United States happens in Florida each year.

A sea turtle's flippers are like paddles, used for steering while swimming. Females also use their flippers for digging nests in the sand.

The Kemp's ridley is the only sea turtle species that nests during the daytime.

Sea turtle hatchlings have a tooth that helps them crack open their eggs when they are ready to hatch. They lose this sharp egg tooth soon after birth.

Scientists have discovered that sea turtles use Earth's magnetic field to find their way back to the beach where they were born.

Leatherbacks have been on Earth longer than any other sea turtle. They have been swimming Earth's oceans for 100 million years.

It takes 20 to 30 years for most sea turtles to become full-grown adults.

The eggs of hawksbill sea turtles are about the size of Ping-Pong balls.

Sea turtle nest

ONLY ABOUT 1 IN 1,000 SEA TURTLE HATCHLINGS LIVES TO BE AN ADULT BECAUSE THE YOUNG TURTLES ARE PREY FOR ANIMALS SUCH AS BIRDS, CRABS, AND FISH.

There are two main groups of sea turtle: The family Dermochelyidae only has one species, the leatherback. The family Cheloniidae includes the six other species.

Sea turtles have good underwater vision, but they can't see well on land.

The sea turtle species are among the few marine reptile species. The vast majority of reptiles live on land.

Like with all turtles, a sea turtle's shell grows with it, so it's always just the right size.

Baby sea turtles are on their own from the time they hatch.

A leatherback's soft shell allows it to make very deep dives without shattering from the water pressure, which increases at greater depths.

Green sea turtles slow their heart rates to stay underwater for hours at a time. Their hearts can beat as low as one beat every nine minutes.

A group of turtle eggs is called a clutch.

Green sea turtles have more nesting sites than any other sea turtle species.

Hawksbill sea turtles are found in tropical areas of the Atlantic and Pacific Oceans. Usually, they do not swim deeper than 60 feet (18 m).

Some female sea turtles will lay eggs each nesting season until they are about 80 years old.

Flatback sea turtles only live along the northern coast of Australia.

Unlike the other species, Kemp's ridley and olive ridley sea turtles come ashore by the thousands to nest once a month during the same three-to-seven-day period.

Hawksbills are the most endangered sea turtle population in the world.

The eggs of flatback sea turtles are the size of billiard balls.

The Pacific leatherback sea turtle is one fast swimmer. It can reach speeds of up to 22 miles an hour (35 kmh), making it the fastest marine reptile.

Leatherback sea turtles can regulate their body temperature, keeping themselves warm even at great depths where water is frigid.

At the time they hatch, baby green sea turtles are only 2 inches (5 cm) long.

Hawksbill sea turtles have translucent shells.

Meal Time!

- **Most sea turtles eat jellyfish.**

- Each species of sea turtle has a unique diet made up a particular mix of prey that no other species of sea turtle eats.

- **Leatherbacks eat about 140 pounds (65 kg) of food in a day.**

- Green sea turtles are herbivores. They eat mainly seagrasses and algae.

- **The jaws of loggerheads are so strong they can crack open and eat hard-shelled prey such as conchs.**

- Green sea turtles improve the health of seagrass beds by eating off the top of the seagrass. This helps the seagrass grow faster, which keeps their biome in balance.

- **The Kemp's ridley sea turtle has a triangular shaped head and hooked beak, which helps it eat crabs, shrimp, and mollusks.**

- Each species of sea turtle has a unique beak that is specifically adapted to the type of prey that it eats.

- **Sea turtles grow algae on their shells. This is a perfect meal for fish such as yellow tang that eat the algae right off the turtle's shell.**

Green sea turtles swimming off the coast of Oahu, Hawaii

BUTTERFLIES NEED SUNLIGHT TO WARM THEIR WINGS SO THEY CAN FLY.

The underside of the wing of a Cramer's eighty-eight butterfly is black, white, and bright red, with a unique pattern that looks like the number 88.

Winging It

Butterflies don't have lungs.

Butterflies live for about two weeks to one year, depending on the species.

Butterflies are insects.

Butterflies make a special glue-like substance that they use to stick their eggs to plants.

It takes about 8 to 12 days for a caterpillar to transform into a butterfly in its chrysalis.

When a butterfly first emerges from its chrysalis, its wings are soft and wet. Soon after, they dry and harden, and then the butterfly is ready to flutter away.

The Queen Alexandra's birdwing butterfly has a wingspan of about one foot (30 cm), making it the largest butterfly on Earth.

The western pygmy blue is one of the smallest butterfly species, with a wingspan of only about 0.4 to 0.8 inches (1–2 cm).

Butterflies drink nectar from flowers, which gives them the energy they need to fly.

Many butterfly species rely on one type of plant as a food for their larvae. For example, milkweed is a monarch larvae's main food source. Without it, they can't survive.

To get the minerals they need, some butterflies sip water from muddy puddles.

There are about 17,500 species of butterflies.

Glasswing butterflies have transparent wings.

Caterpillars shed their skin at least four times while developing. Each molt often changes the color and appearance of the caterpillar.

Butterflies taste with their feet.

The plants that a caterpillar eats help it grow the tissues it needs to transform into a butterfly during metamorphosis.

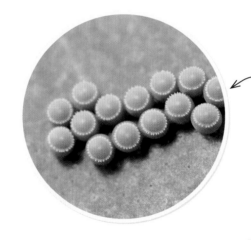

← Eggs

Adult

Caterpillar

Chrysalis →

Adult emerging from its chrysalis

FOUR STAGES MAKE UP THE LIFE CYCLE OF A BUTTERFLY: EGG, CATERPILLAR, CHRYSALIS, AND ADULT.

BUTTERFLIES HAVE A PROBOSCIS, A LONG TONGUELIKE TUBE USED TO DRINK NECTAR AND OTHER LIQUIDS.

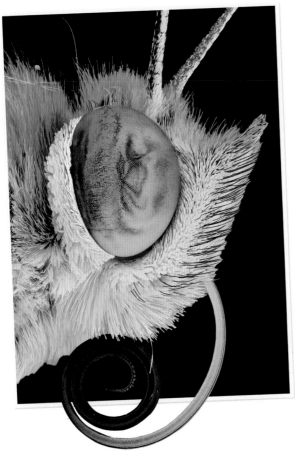

Blue morpho

Painted lady butterflies live in more places around the world than any other species. They are found everywhere except Australia and Antarctica.

Butterflies may eat rotting fruit and even dung.

Some butterfly species rely on ants to protect their larvae. These butterflies release special chemicals that attract the ants to the larvae.

A butterfly assembles its own proboscis from two separate body parts.

Some species of butterflies hibernate.

Though blue morpho butterflies are known for their bright coloring, underneath their wings these insects are brown with spots. The spots resemble eyes and help keep predators away.

Some male butterflies perform a special mating dance when trying to attract a mate.

To get the sodium they need, some butterflies drink the tears of turtles.

Blue morpho butterflies live in the rain forests of Central and South America. They spend most of their time on shrubs or the forest floor.

Butterflies don't sleep, but they do rest with their eyes open.

Butterflies can't chew, so they drink their meals.

Some butterflies migrate.

Butterflies cannot fly if it's colder than 55°F (13°C).

As soon as they emerge from the chrysalis, most female butterflies are ready to mate.

Some butterflies use bright, bold colors and patterns to warn predators that they're toxic.

Once a caterpillar is in its chrysalis, it turns into a soupy liquid before it transforms into a butterfly.

Butterflies do not have eyelids.

Butterflies have the ability to see colors that humans can't. They can also see ultraviolet light.

The spots on the underside of the blue morpho butterfly help keep predators away because they look like staring eyes.

Magnificent Monarchs

- In the fall, monarch butterflies migrate—travel—up to 3,000 miles (4,800 km) from Canada and the United States south to parts of Southern California and Mexico.

- **Monarchs are the only butterflies that make such a long migration.**

- Only male monarch butterflies have one black dot on each hind wing.

- **Monarch butterflies beat their wings about 5 to 12 times a second.**

- One monarch butterfly egg is about the size of a pinhead.

Butterflies rest hanging upside down.

Skipper butterflies can fly at speeds of up to 37 miles an hour (60 kph).

When it rains, butterflies have been observed finding shelter under leaves.

On the outside of their bodies, butterflies have exoskeletons, which protect them from drying out.

When its wings are closed, the dead leaf butterfly looks just like—well—a dead leaf. When its wings open, this butterfly displays a very colorful pattern.

The Saint Francis' satyr butterfly lives near the Fort Bragg military base in North Carolina and nowhere else in the world.

Butterflies use their antennae for balance and to smell the world around them.

Monarch caterpillar

Take a Big Bite

Great white shark attacking a seagull

49 Totally Random Facts About SHARKS

Shark embryos attack each other in the womb. • **Due to the unique shape of their heads and the placement of their eyes, a hammerhead has a wider field of vision than any other kind of shark.** • The longest fish in the world is the whale shark. • **Male great whites and bull sharks are smaller than females.** • Not all sharks live in the ocean. Some can live in freshwater lakes and rivers. • **Spiny dogfish sharks are pregnant for two years.** • Great white sharks have a more powerful bite than jungle cats. • **Bull sharks bite harder for their size than great whites.** • Bull sharks start their attack by head-butting their prey • **Lightning strikes are more deadly than shark attacks.** • Hippos, deer, and cows are more deadly than sharks. • **Females of some shark species can reproduce without male sharks.** • Blue shark litters can contain up to 135 pups. • **Shark skeletons aren't made of bone.** • Most sharks need to keep swimming to stay alive. • **Cookie cutter sharks have lips like suction cups. They grab onto prey and take a bite, leaving a cookie-shaped hole in their**

victim. • Sharks have been on Earth longer than the period of time dinosaurs existed. • **Sharks used to be bigger than a four-story building.** • Sharks have up to 15 rows of teeth in each jaw. • **Unlike humans, sharks have a never-ending supply of new teeth.** • A diver in Florida found a shark tooth bigger than his hand. • **Sharkskin is covered in toothlike scales called denticles.** • The dwarf lantern shark is so small it can fit in your hand. • **Great whites can detect**

OF ALL THE SHARKS, HAMMERHEAD SHARKS HAVE THE KEENEST ABILITY FIND PREY BECAUSE OF THEIR UNIQUE HEAD SHAPE WITH WIDE-SET EYES.

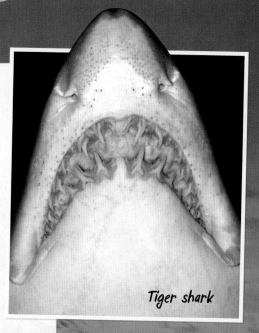

Angelshark

THE WHALE SHARK'S MOUTH OPENS 4 FEET (1.2 M) WIDE.

blood one-third of a mile (0.53 km) away. • Brown-banded bamboo shark embryos can sense danger. • **Humans and sharks share a common ancestor.** • Scientists discovered a 120-million-year-old shark fossil. • **Like tree rings, a shark's vertebrae, or bones, tell its age.** • Sharks have an inner ear that detects not only sounds, but also gravity and acceleration. • **Great whites are named for their white underbellies.** • Some sharks heat their eyes to improve their vision. • **Unlike most animals, sharks can move both the top and bottom jaws.** • The skin on whale sharks is 6 inches (15 cm) thick. • **The majority of sharks give birth to fully grown offspring. The others lay eggs.**
• Baby sharks are born with all of their teeth. • **There are over 500 species of**

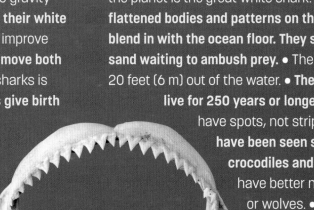

shark. • Though whale sharks are gigantic, scientists believe they can survive for weeks with little or no food. • **Unlike most sharks, hammerheads sometimes like to swim in schools.** • The largest predatory fish on the planet is the great white shark. • **Angelsharks have flattened bodies and patterns on their skin that help them blend in with the ocean floor. They stay hidden under the sand waiting to ambush prey.** • The mako shark can leap 20 feet (6 m) out of the water. • **The Greenland shark can live for 250 years or longer.** • Baby tiger sharks have spots, not stripes. • **Tiger sharks have been seen sharing food with crocodiles and great whites.** • Sharks have better night vision than cats or wolves. • **A shark's tongue is called a basihyal.** • The shortfin mako shark can swim 46 miles (74 km) an hour in short bursts.

THAT'S SO RANDOM:

Sharks Have a Sixth Sense!

SHARKS HAVE SOME AMAZING ABILITIES. Their sense of smell is so keen that they can detect **a single drop of blood** in an Olympic-size swimming pool. Some species have jaws so powerful that they can bite down three to four times harder than a lion or tiger. And sharks have another secret weapon—**they can detect electric fields** in the water. How? Sharks have a special network of cells called electroreceptors. Tiny holes on their heads and snouts connect to narrow canals filled with a jellylike substance. The canals end in a gel-filled bulb lined with special cells that can detect changes of electricity in the jellylike substance. These cells send messages through nerves to a shark's brain, which allow the shark to detect tiny changes in electricity in seawater produced by fish. Since all living fish create their own electrical fields, these **subtle signals can lead them to find prey.** Sharks can even detect fish hiding under the sand. One species, the hammerhead, has more than 3,000 of these special pores, making it a super-sensor among sharks. The unusual shape of the broad, flat head enables the shark to broaden its search for prey.

Tiger shark

Puppy Love

58 Totally Random Facts About DOGS

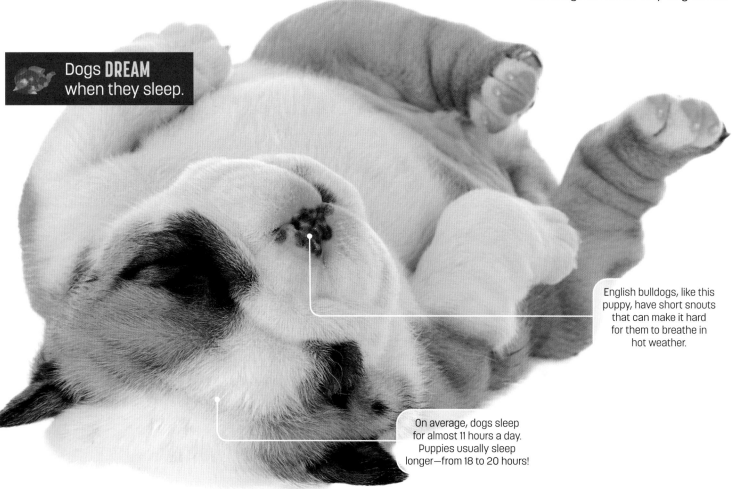

An Australian cattle dog (right) with its buddy

In a long-distance race, a greyhound would beat a cheetah.

All puppies are born deaf, blind, and toothless.

The United States is home to more pet dogs than any other country.

Studies have shown that dogs can learn over 100 words and gestures.

In a court of law, a bloodhound's sense of smell can be used to help identify a person who has committed a crime.

The world's tallest dog was a Great Dane named Zeus. He was 44 inches (112 cm) tall.

For at least 30 years in a row, the Labrador retriever has been on the American Kennel Club's top 10 list of most popular dog breeds. That's the longest run for any dog breed.

Dogs **DREAM** when they sleep.

English bulldogs, like this puppy, have short snouts that can make it hard for them to breathe in hot weather.

On average, dogs sleep for almost 11 hours a day. Puppies usually sleep longer—from 18 to 20 hours!

Dogs use 18 muscles to move their ears.

Each dog has its own unique noseprint, sort of like a human fingerprint.

There are 197 different dog breeds recognized by the American Kennel Club.

Basenjis don't bark—they yodel, whine, or scream.

Thanks to his guide dog, Orient, a blind man was able to hike the Appalachian Trail for eight months.

On average, 30 percent of Dalmatians are deaf in one ear.

Dogs pant to cool down. The only place where dogs sweat like humans is on their paws.

If a Dalmatian has larger dark patches, it's less likely to be deaf.

The saluki dog breed was the pet of ancient Egyptian royalty.

A group of dogs go for a walk in New York City.

Similar to humans, dogs can be right-pawed or left-pawed.

Despite the name, the Australian shepherd was originally bred in the United States.

Unlike most dog breeds, Chow Chows and Shar-Peis have blue-black tongues.

Dogs have three eyelids to keep their eyes moist and protected.

The part of a dog's brain that detects different smells is about 40 times larger than the same part in a human's brain.

When sending holiday cards, 70 percent of people include their dog's name.

A German shepherd named Rin Tin Tin was a famous movie star in the 1920s.

Dogs sniff each other's behinds to say hello.

According to a study, the shape of a dog's head affects its personality.

Dogs have been trained to help track rhino poachers in South Africa.

A labrador puppy. labradors are the most popular dogs in the U.S.

A DOG'S NOSE HAS ABOUT 300 MILLION RECEPTORS TO HELP IT SMELL. A HUMAN NOSE HAS ABOUT 5 MILLION.

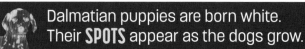 Dalmatian puppies are born white. Their **SPOTS** appear as the dogs grow.

Despite its name, the Labrador retriever didn't originate in Labrador, which is on the Canadian mainland, but rather on the Canadian island of Newfoundland.

Dogs use their ears to communicate with humans and other dogs.

A "beagler" is the name for a person who hunts with a beagle.

It's a myth that dogs are completely color-blind. They can see yellow and blue.

With water-resistant coats and webbed feet, Newfoundlands are excellent swimmers.

Dogs have about 1,700 taste buds, while humans average 9,000 taste buds.

After they go to the bathroom, dogs kick backward to mark their territory with the scent glands in their paws.

Some dogs can detect medical conditions like cancer.

In 2016, a brave Newfoundland named Whizz saved nine people from drowning.

Dogs can hear sounds from farther away than people can.

When sleeping, dogs curl up in a ball to protect themselves. It's an instinct they still have from their ancestors that lived in the wild.

Some dogs are as smart as a two-year-old kid.

Wet noses help dogs smell better.

Dogs can sniff and breathe at the same time.

Petting a dog is good for your health—it can reduce blood pressure.

A black labrador retriever fetches a toy from the water.

Border collies are one of the most intelligent dog breeds.

Dogs Are Kind!

ACCORDING TO A STUDY CONDUCTED IN 2015, DOGS HAVE DEMONSTRATED THAT THEY CAN BE KIND. Just as you might share a favorite treat with a sibling or buddy, it turns out dogs will do the same. In scientist-speak, this is called pro-social behavior and it is rare, or at least hard to show, outside of humans. In the study, 16 dogs were trained to do several experiments where the dog could move a bar that would deliver a treat to the dog next to them without getting a treat themselves. **To their surprise, dogs shared treats, especially with dogs they were familiar with.** Scientists aren't sure whether this tendency to be nice is instinctual from the days when dogs were wolves living in the wild, or if the dogs learned to share because they've been domesticated and living with people. **Either way, these pups are paw-sitively awesome!**

Dogs wag their tails to the right to show they're happy.

"Frito feet" can happen when sweat and bacteria build up in your pup's paws. It makes their paws smell like corn chips.

Scientists think dogs like to poop facing north or south. They twirl before they go to orient themselves.

More than half of all U.S. presidents owned dogs.

Stray dogs in Russia learned how to ride the subway.

Dogs are related to wolves.

There are about 900 million dogs in the world.

The world's oldest dog, an Australian cattle dog named Bluey, lived to be 29.

A golden retriever named Max was the mayor of a small California, U.S.A., town.

Dogs sometimes yawn to calm themselves.

JUST LIKE WITH HUMANS, YAWNING IS CONTAGIOUS FOR DOGS. DOGS SOMETIMES YAWN WHEN THEY SEE HUMANS DO IT FIRST.

IN THE UNITED STATES, ABOUT HALF OF ALL DOG OWNERS SNOOZE WITH THEIR FURRY FRIENDS.

Bats, including this gray long-eared bat, have great hearing. Their hearing helps with echolocation—sensing sound waves—which they use to find their way around and to locate prey.

A bat's eyes are adapted to the night, the time most bat's hunt prey. Along with great hearing, their sight aids in the hunt.

Nocturnal Navigators

63 Totally Random Facts About BATS

Some bat species live in groups called colonies, and some species live alone.

Bats can be found in deserts, forests, farms, and even in cities.

Bats are the only mammals that can fly.

Bats belong to the order Chiroptera, which means "hand wing" in Greek.

There are more than 1,400 species of bats.

Bats are found all over the world except in the Arctic, Antarctic, and on some remote islands.

Bats have been around for at least 50 million years.

Most bats are nocturnal.

Bats have webbed wings.

Most bats use echolocation to navigate and locate prey. A bat sends out a sound and an echo bounces back, telling the bat about the location of objects around it.

A bat hanging upside down, eating a grasshopper

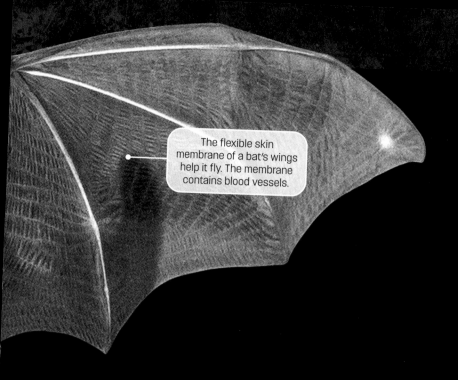

The flexible skin membrane of a bat's wings help it fly. The membrane contains blood vessels.

Some bats produce sound through their noses.

Many bat species are color-blind.

Some bats purr, click, and buzz.

Flying foxes have been observed swimming.

Some bats use their feet to snatch prey.

Some carnivorous bat species eat frogs, lizards, and birds.

Vampire bats consume the blood of cattle, horses, and deer, not of humans.

Some bats vibrate when they rest.

Some bats have suction pads that help them stay in place.

Unlike the majority of bat species, the sucker-footed bat rests right side up instead of upside down.

Bats are extremely clean and groom themselves for hours.

Vampire bats not only groom themselves—they also lend a hand to groom other bats in their group.

Male and female bats roost separately except when mating.

Some bats can live to be more than 20 years old.

Bats are pollinators. More than 300 species of fruit depend on bats for pollination, including avocados, bananas, and mangoes.

Bat poop, known as guano, is sometimes used as fertilizer.

The Mexican free-tailed bat can fly as high as 10,000 feet (3,050 m).

There are two main categories of bats: megabats and microbats.

SOME SPECIES OF FRUIT BATS, ALSO KNOWN AS FLYING FOXES, CAN HAVE A WINGSPAN OF 5 FEET (1.5 M).

Vampire bat

The Kitti's hog-nosed bat, also known as the bumblebee bat, is about the size of a thumbnail and weighs less than a penny.

Bats can survive being encrusted in ice when they hibernate.

Some bats fly up to 250 miles (400 km) in a single night.

Suction pads

Madagascar sucker-footed bat

BATS HAVE BELLY BUTTONS, JUST LIKE HUMANS.

ONE OF EVERY FIVE mammals living on the planet is a bat.

The tube-lipped nectar bat is only about 2 inches (5 cm) long but has a tongue that is 3 inches (7.5 cm) long!

Bats are responsible for pollinating up to 50 percent of the vegetation in the forests of Asia, Africa, and Europe.

One bat can eat up to 1,200 mosquitoes in a single hour.

Only three species of bats feed on blood.

Vampire bats don't suck blood; they lick it from a small bite they make in their prey.

Bats are immune to many diseases that can be lethal to humans.

The smallest microbat, and the world's smallest mammal by length, is the bumblebee bat.

Not all bats hibernate.

When the weather cools, some bat species survive by migrating to warmer areas in search of food.

Bats have few natural predators—only owls, hawks, and snakes prey on them.

Bats can fly as high as 10,000 feet (3,050 m).

Honduran white bats fold leaves into little tents that they use for shelter and protection from predators.

A colony of bats flying out at sunset to feed

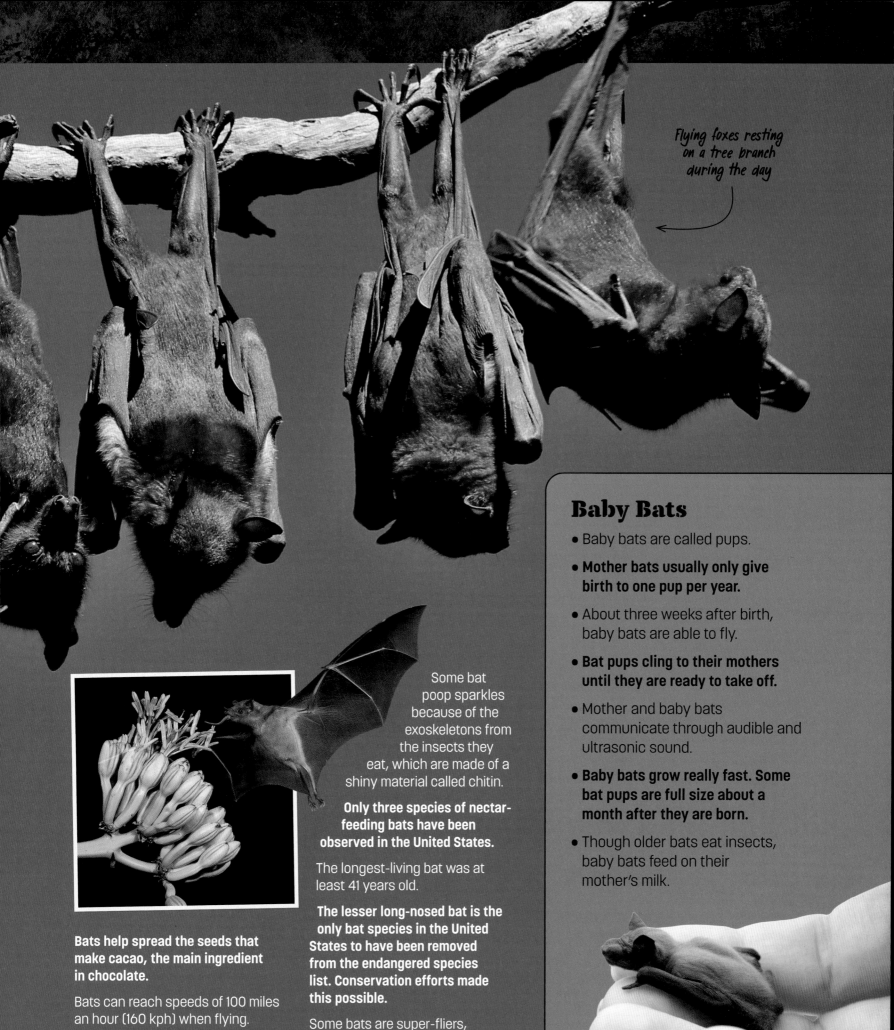

Flying foxes resting on a tree branch during the day

Baby Bats

- Baby bats are called pups.

- **Mother bats usually only give birth to one pup per year.**

- About three weeks after birth, baby bats are able to fly.

- **Bat pups cling to their mothers until they are ready to take off.**

- Mother and baby bats communicate through audible and ultrasonic sound.

- **Baby bats grow really fast. Some bat pups are full size about a month after they are born.**

- Though older bats eat insects, baby bats feed on their mother's milk.

Some bat poop sparkles because of the exoskeletons from the insects they eat, which are made of a shiny material called chitin.

Only three species of nectar-feeding bats have been observed in the United States.

The longest-living bat was at least 41 years old.

The lesser long-nosed bat is the only bat species in the United States to have been removed from the endangered species list. Conservation efforts made this possible.

Some bats are super-fliers, reaching speeds of more than 60 miles an hour (96 kmh).

Bats help spread the seeds that make cacao, the main ingredient in chocolate.

Bats can reach speeds of 100 miles an hour (160 kph) when flying.

Each night a bat can eat its body weight in insects.

Elephants are capable of feeling deep emotion and show joy, grief, anger, and love.

Female elephants can be pregnant for up to 22 months, or almost two years!

Elephants have about 40,000 different muscles in their trunks.

Elephant tusks never stop growing.

An Asian elephant can pick up and open a peanut shell using its trunk.

An elephant's trunk can hold up to 2 gallons (7.5 L) of water.

When underwater, elephants use their trunks like a snorkel.

Just like humans can be right-handed or left-handed, elephants can be right-tusked or left-tusked.

It takes about two years for young elephants to start growing tusks.

Elephants stomp their feet to signal that danger is near.

Elephants use their tusks to pull bark off trees and dig up roots for food.

Female elephants have one baby every four to five years.

On most of its body, an elephant's skin is an inch (2.5 cm) thick.

The folds and wrinkles in an elephant's skin help it hold water, which keeps the animal cool.

To protect their skin from the sun, elephants take dust and mud baths.

Elephants spend three-quarters of their day eating.

Elephants eat up to 330 pounds (150 kg) of food per day.

Elephants are the world's largest land animal.

Male elephants reach their full size between 35 and 40 years old.

Elephants can live for 60 to 70 years in the wild.

Baby elephants can weigh as much as 265 pounds (120 kg) at birth.

Baby elephants are called calves.

There are three species of elephant: African savanna elephant, African forest elephant, and Asian elephant.

Mammoth Mammals

69 Totally Random Facts About ELEPHANTS

Trumpet calls, body language, touch, and smell, are all ways elephants communicate.

Elephants are born blind.

An elephant calf can stand within 20 minutes of birth.

Baby elephants can walk within an hour of being born. After two days they can keep up with the herd.

Elephants have excellent memories.

African and Asian elephants are both endangered.

ELEPHANTS CAN'T JUMP.

Female elephants and their calves live in groups with a female leader.

Elephant dung can be made into paper.

There are no bones in the elephant's trunk.

If an elephant dies, other elephants in the herd will explore the bones, touching them and standing close by.

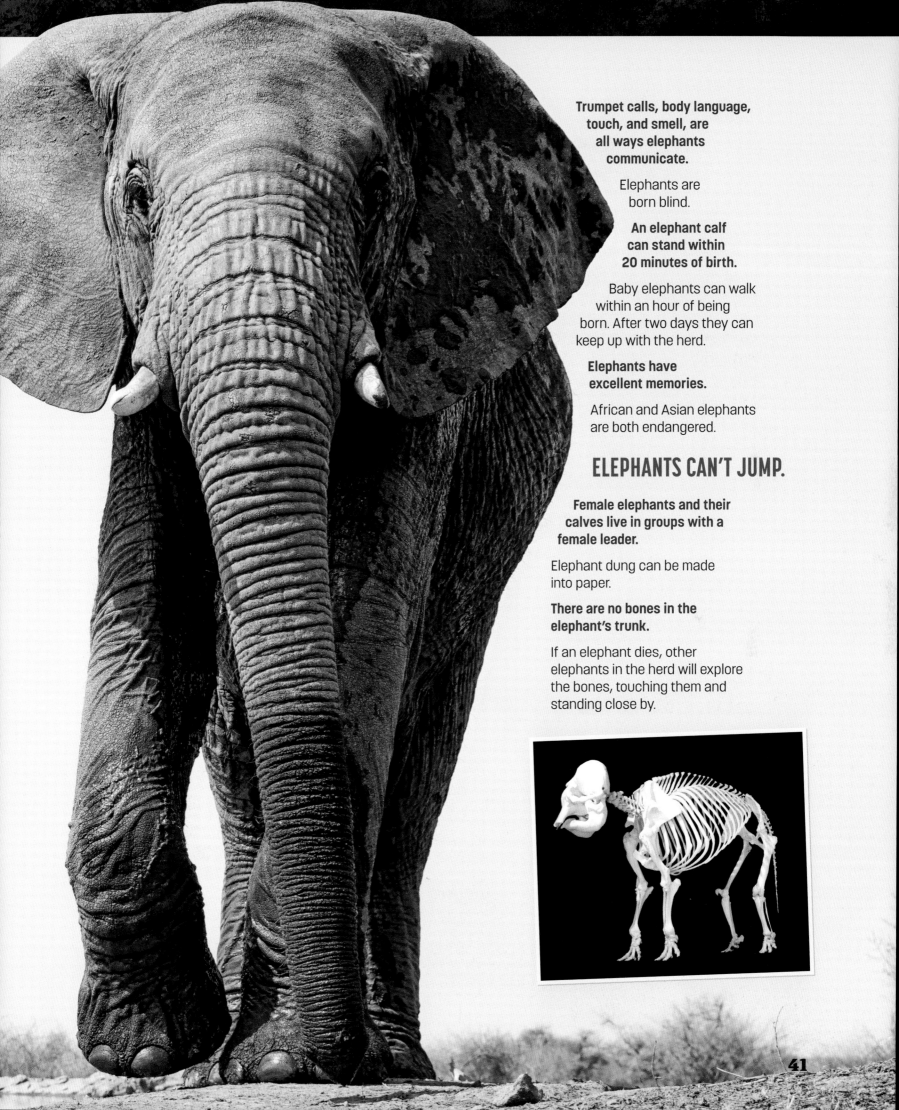

THE AVERAGE ADULT ELEPHANT POOPS 220 POUNDS (100 KG) A DAY.

In a single day, elephants can drink 40 gallons (151 L) of water.

Elephants can smell water up to 12 miles (19 km) away.

Elephants can swim for long distances.

An elephant's heart rate is very low, about 27 beats per minute.

Elephants only sleep for about two hours a night.

Like horses and giraffes, elephants can sleep while standing.

Only some male Asian elephants have tusks.

Elephants use their fingerlike projections at the end of their trunks to scratch itchy skin behind their ears and wipe dust from their eyes.

An elephant sucks in water with its trunk, then empties the water in its mouth to drink.

African and Asian elephants migrate and walk the same routes each year.

Both male and female African elephants grow tusks.

African forest elephants live in the forests of Africa's Congo Basin.

Elephants spend 12 to 18 hours a day eating grass, plants, and fruit.

In Mount Elgon National Park in Kenya, a group of elephants use tusks to mine for salt in underground caves.

A herd of Asian elephants walked 300 miles (480 km) across China, the longest known distance traveled by elephants in the country.

Elephants can recognize themselves in a mirror.

Female elephants can have babies until they are around 50 years old.

Elephants are afraid of bees.

Baby elephants suck on their trunks for comfort, just like human babies might suck on their thumbs.

Indonesian forestry officials ride elephants as they patrol an area affected by forest fire.

The oldest known elephant lived to be at least 86 years old.

Elephants wrap their trunks together to say hello.

African forest elephants have straighter tusks, darker skin, and rounder ears than African savanna elephants.

Elephants can be trained to fight fires by carrying crews and equipment into remote areas.

Elephant can "catch" yawns from humans.

ELEPHANTS HAVE 5-INCH (13 CM)-LONG EYELASHES, THE LONGEST OF ANY ANIMAL IN THE WORLD.

Like cats, elephants purr to communicate.

The intestines of an elephant can be as long as 60 feet (18 m)—more than half a football field.

An elephant tooth can weigh more than a six-pack of soda cans.

Elephants can learn as many as 60 commands.

- **African elephants have much larger ears than Asian elephants.**

- **Elephants use their ears as air conditioners. They release heat by flapping them.**

- **The ears of African elephants are shaped like the continent where they live—Africa.**

- **Each elephant has completely unique ears.**

- **African elephants use their long ears to signal to each other.**

Sky Hunters

51 Totally Random Facts About BIRDS OF PREY

Andean condor

Birds of prey are meat-eating birds that hunt live animals or eat dead animals, using their feet to grasp their prey. • **Birds of prey are also known as raptors.** • In Latin, *raptor* means "to seize or take by force." • **All birds of prey have two things in common: sharp, hooked beaks and curved claws for snatching prey.** • There are two groups of birds of prey: Falconiformes that hunt during the day, and Strigiformes, or owls, that hunt at night. • **Condors and eagles are some of the largest and strongest of all living birds.** • Condors can live to be more than 50 years old. • **An owl can carry prey that is up to three times its body weight.** • Raptors' ears are covered in feathers and hidden behind their eyes. • **The black-thighed falconet is one of the smallest birds of prey. Native to Southeast Asia, it's only about 6 to 7 inches (15–18 cm) long.** • The largest bird of prey is the Andean condor. Males can weigh as much as 33 pounds (15 kg). • **Birds of prey usually kill with their feet.** • The Egyptian vulture hurls stones with its beak to break ostrich eggs. • **Honey buzzards eat wasp and bee larvae. They dig up insect nests with their talons.** • The bat hawk catches all its food in about 20 minutes each day at dusk. • **Most raptors sleep all night with their heads buried in the feathers of their back or hunched on their shoulders.** • White-tailed kites sometimes live in groups of 100 birds. They are mainly found in Mexico but have a small range in parts of the United States. • **Male sharp-shinned hawks tear off the heads of their prey.** • Bald eagles have been known to snatch fish out of the talons of ospreys. • **Elf owls are the smallest owls in the world. They are only about 5 inches (13 cm) tall.** • An eagle nest in Ohio

Owls, like this European scops owl, have tube-shaped eyes that don't move. They move their whole heads to look around.

An owl's ears are located on the sides of the head and covered by feathers.

THERE ARE MORE THAN 200 SPECIES OF OWLS.

was used for 34 years. Eventually, wind caused the tree to topple over. ● **In addition to eating other birds, peregrine falcons also eat bats.** ● Red-tailed hawks have a very wide range. They are found from Canada to Mexico and live anywhere from deserts to woodlands. ● **A Cooper's hawk squeezes its prey until the animal is dead. Sometimes it will even drown its prey.** ● Ospreys are the only hawks in North America to eat an almost all-fish diet. ● **Red-shouldered hawks shoot their droppings over the edge of their nests.** ● Rough-legged hawks have been known to use caribou bones to build their nests. ● **A flock of broad-winged hawks is called a kettle. These birds fly in large groups from North America to South America in the fall.** ● Swainson's hawks migrate more than 6,000 miles (9,650 km) from Canada to Argentina, flying an average of 124 miles (200 km) a day. ● **People have relied on birds of prey for thousands of years to help them hunt small animals.** ● Sam Wilson, or the Marvel hero Captain America, was formerly named after a bird of prey: the Falcon. ● **Female rulers throughout history have participated in falconry—or the sport of hunting with falcons—including Queen Elizabeth I, Catherine the Great of Russia, and Mary, Queen of Scots.** ● To attract a mate, a male golden eagle dives and swoops multiple times in a display known as "sky-dancing." ● **Birds of prey have an extra eyelid that protects their eyes as they dive.** ● When the weather gets cold, condors can raise their neck feathers for warmth. ● **Female California condors only lay one egg during nesting season.** ● The bald eagle became the national symbol of the United States in 1792. ● **The heavy use of pesticides nearly killed off bald eagles. Thanks to conservation efforts, the birds have made a comeback.** ● Bald eagles lay two or three eggs at a time. It takes about 36 days for the eggs to hatch. ● **Baby bald eagles fly at about six weeks old.** ● Snowy owls are diurnal, meaning they are active during the day. Most owl species are nocturnal, or active at night. ● **The snowy owl's preferred food is lemmings. It can eat more than 1,500 lemmings a year.**

Talons

Fearsome Falcons

- Falcons have a tooth on the end of their beak.

- **Instead of squeezing their prey, falcons usually kill prey by biting.**

- Peregrine falcons can dive at speeds of more than 200 miles (322 kmh) an hour.

- **Spotting prey from a distance is second nature to falcons. They can see eight times better than humans.**

- Falcons have one mating partner for life.

- **Peregrine falcons migrate more than 15,000 miles (24,100 km) a year.**

THAT'S SO RANDOM:

Fastest Animal on Earth!

THE PEREGRINE FALCON IS NOT ONLY THE FASTEST BIRD BUT ALSO THE FASTEST MEMBER OF THE ANIMAL WORLD. This bird could beat a cheetah and a greyhound in a sprinting contest. Also known as the duck hawk, the peregrine is the most powerful species of falcon. The peregrine falcon is a bird of prey, also known as a raptor, which is a type of bird that mainly uses its talons to seize prey like snack-size birds mid-flight. Peregrine falcons are some of the world's most common birds of prey. **They live on every continent but Antarctica.** The fast fliers can be found everywhere from tundra to deserts and even cities, but they prefer open spaces and thrive near coasts. **How is this raptor able to dive at a speed of 242 miles an hour (389 kmh)?** The bird has special adaptations that make it a natural-born jet engine. The flapping strength is due to a very large keel, which is a ridge on their breastbone where the muscles attach, allowing extra muscle power. This bird also has a pointed aerodynamic shape, with swept-back wings. **Its nostrils are specially adapted to help it breathe as it dives,** and it has binocular vision eight times sharper than a human's.

Web Masters

50 Totally Random Facts About *SPIDERS*

Black widow

THE FEMALE SOUTHERN BLACK WIDOW SPIDER HANGS UPSIDE DOWN IN HER WEB TO SHOW THE RED MARK ON HER UNDERSIDE. THIS MARK IS A WARNING FOR PREDATORS TO STAY AWAY.

Some jumping spiders can see lights that humans can't detect.

Just like a porcupine, some tarantulas can fling tiny, sharp hairs at predators to scare them off.

Some spiders form groups of thousands to make large webs and share the catch.

The ogre-faced spider spins a netlike web to scoop up prey.

Bolas spiders go fishing for moths by spinning a long line of silk with a sticky bottom.

Spiders help plants grow.

A wolf spider's six eyes give it excellent night vision, helping it hunt insects under the cover of darkness.

Spiders eat many pesky insects.

Spiders are not insects. Insects have six legs, whereas spiders have eight legs.

Baby spiders are called spiderlings.

Not all spiders spin webs. Some spiders chase their prey.

Some spiders have fangs that eject venom.

Though most spiders have eight eyes, they can't see very well. They use hair on their body to feel their way around.

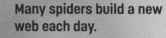
Jumping spider

Many spiders build a new web each day.

Huntsman spiders in Madagascar eat tree frogs. Scientists think they make traps using leaves and spider silk to lure in their prey before taking a bite.

Some spiders eat their webs when they're done with them.

Spiders are part of a group called arachnids.

There are more than 45,000 known species of spiders.

The Himalayan jumping spider's scientific name is *Euophrys omnisuperstes*, which means "standing above everything." This is fitting for a spider that has been found living at elevations of up to 22,000 feet (6,700 m).

The bird-dung crab spider of Southeast Asia looks like bird poop, and it even stinks. It's the perfect way to both lure in prey and keep predators away.

There are different kinds of spiderwebs, including orbs, funnels, and sheets.

Almost all spiders are carnivores, but the Bagheera kiplingi is unique among spiders because it eats mostly plants.

It takes a spider about an hour to build a web.

The wolf spider makes a hole in the ground and waits inside to ambush its prey.

The spruce-fir moss spider creates tube-shaped webs.

Funnel-web spider in its tube-shaped web

Most spiders that build webs are called orb weavers, because the web is a round spiral.

When a spider lays eggs, she protects them by storing them in a sac she makes from silk.

Wolf spiders carry their egg sacs. When the eggs hatch, the babies sit on the spider's back.

Some spiders trap their prey in a cocoon of silk, then inject venom into it.

Spiders can see colors that human can't.

Some spiders fish.

Some spiders mimic ants to evade predators.

Some spiders have no eyes, and some have 12.

Almost all spiders have venom.

Only about 25 spider species carry venom that's harmful to humans.

Arachnophobia is the fear of spiders.

A spider in Australia is nicknamed "*Sparklemuffin*."

Jumping spiders can jump up to 50 times the length of their bodies.

Wonderous Silk

- **Spiders spin silk from glands called spinnerets.**

- Tarantulas can make silk with their feet.

- **Spiders can make as many as seven different kinds of silk for their webs.**

- Some spiders use their silk to float in the air—a process called ballooning.

- **Spider silk is stronger than steel.**

Some spiders create pulley systems with silk to hoist their prey off the ground.

The happy-face spider looks like a tiny smiley face.

Some spiders can catch and eat bats.

Dracula spiders in Australia have red fangs.

Diving bell spiders can create air bubbles to breathe underwater.

The world's largest spider is the **GOLIATH BIRDEATER TARANTULA,** which catches and eats birds.

WHEN A HORSE
APPEARS TO BE
LAUGHING, IT
MIGHT ACTUALLY
BE TRYING TO
TASTE SOMETHING
IN THE AIR.

Horsing Around

97 Totally Random Facts About HORSES

A newborn horse is called a foal. • **A foal can walk about two hours after birth.** • Horses live about 25 to 30 years. • **The oldest horse on record lived to be 62. His name was Old Billy.** • Horses have 205 bones. • **People started keeping horses more about 6,000 years ago.** • Horses are herbivores. They mainly eat grass, grain, and hay. • **Horses have bigger eyes than any other land mammal.** • Because their eyes are located on the sides of their heads, horses can see nearly 360 degrees around them. • **The typical horse can gallop at 35 miles an hour (48 kmh).** • A racehorse named Secretariat set a record for running when he ran 1.5 miles (2.4 km) in 144 seconds in 1973. • **Shetland ponies were once used to haul coal from coal mines. They were given the nickname "pit ponies."** • The Arabian is the oldest horse breed. It can be traced back to about 3000 B.C. That's about 5,000 years! • **A male horse is called a** stallion. • A female horse is called a mare. • **A young male horse is called a colt.** • A young female horse is called a filly. • **Ponies are a smaller breed of horse. They have shorter legs and thicker necks.** • Compared with horses, ponies have thicker coats, manes, and tails. • **A horse tail is mainly used to keep away insects.** • A horse can lose up to 1 cup (0.25 L) of blood a day from insect bites. Its tail helps keeps insects away. • **Some miniature horses serve as service animals to people with disabilities.** • Hackney ponies were first bred to pull carriages. Now, they are mainly show ponies. • **The eohippus was an ancient ancestor of modern horses. It lived about 55 million years ago.** •

FOR THEIR SIZE, SHETLAND PONIES ARE THE STRONGEST OF ALL HORSE BREEDS. THEY CAN PULL TWICE THEIR BODY WEIGHT.

Horse hooves are made of keratin, the same substance as human fingernails and hair. • **Horses express their moods with their ears and eyes and by flaring their nostrils.** • Horses twist their ears around to tune into different sounds. • **Horses express anger by moving their ears back.** • Horses are related to donkeys and zebras. • **Horses have a better** sense of smell than humans do. • Horses can't breathe through their mouths, only through their nostrils. • **Horses with pink skin can get sunburned, just like humans.** • To tell if a horse is cold, feel behind its ears. If the backs of the ears are cold, the horse is too. • **A horse will mourn the loss of a companion.** • Clydesdale horses have long hair around their hooves and ankles. This feature is called "feathering." • **Horses have a third eyelid.** • Adult male horses have 40 teeth; females only have 36. • **In a horse's head, the teeth take up more space than the brain.** • The longest horse tail on record belonged to a mare. Her tail measured more than 12 feet (3.6 m). • **Horses can't vomit.** • Horses produce

← Zebra   ← Donkey

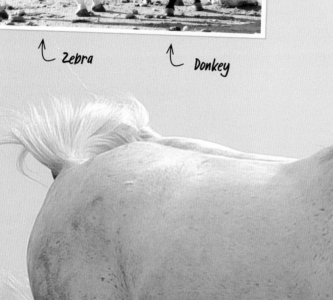

about 10 gallons (39 L) of saliva a day. ● **The Guinness World Record for the tallest horse goes to Big Jake, standing nearly 83 inches (210 cm) tall.** ● There were no horses in Australia until 1788. ● **It's possible to estimate a horse's age by looking at its teeth.** ● Horses don't have collarbones. Muscles and ligaments connect their shoulders to their skeletons. ● **When foals are born, their hooves are covered with soft, slipper-like tissue to prevent harming the mother at birth.** ● Dressage is a form of horseback riding where a horse and rider perform precise moves, sometimes to music. ● **Young horses usually learn by observing their mothers in the first few months of life.** ● Although humans have just 3 ear muscles, horses have 10. ● **A horse's heart is about the size of a basketball.** ● A farrier is someone who specializes in taking care of horse hooves, including making and placing horseshoes. ● **A hippophile is someone who loves horses.** ● Horses nibble each other with their teeth as a way of grooming. ● **There are more than 350 breeds of horses and ponies around the world.** ● In the wild, one horse will stand guard while the others sleep in order to watch for predators. ● **The world's smallest horse breed is the Falabella. These horses are about the size of a large dog.** ● Horses have two tiny blind spots, one directly in front of them and one directly behind. ● **The shortest horse on record is Thumbelina. She was a miniature horse that stood just 17.5 inches (44.5 cm) tall.** ● Mustangs are feral horses that live in the grasslands of the American West. ● **Horses belong to a group of animals called ungulates, animals with hooves.** ● Some early horses had toes. ● **A mother horse can identify her baby by the baby's unique scent.** ● Horse height is measured in units of "hands." Traditionally, the width of a man's hand, one hand is equal to 4 inches (10 cm). ● **Horses are measured at the spot where the neck meets the back, which is known as the withers.**

Gypsy Vanner horses can grow **MUSTACHES.**

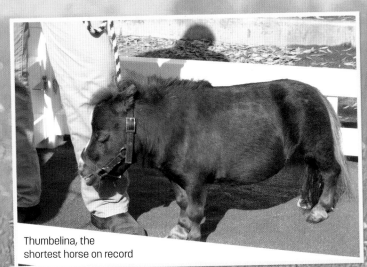

Thumbelina, the shortest horse on record

A horse's hooves keep growing throughout its life. They get ground down by walking. • **Horses can rotate their ears 180 degrees.** • Horses communicate by whinnying, snorting, and neighing and by using facial gestures. • Horses can't burp. • **Mysteriously, horses and camels disappeared from North America about 12,000 years ago.** • The only continent without horses is Antarctica. • **All horses graze on grass for 13 to 18 hours a day.** • Humans first tamed horses about 6,000 years ago in central Asia. • **A Spanish explorer first brought horses to the American continent in the 1500s.** • In the wild, horses live in herds with 3 to 20 others. • **Herds of wild horses usually have several mares and foals and one to four male stallions.** • Lipizzaner stallions are known for their graceful dancing and jumping abilities. • **Przewalski's horses are wild horses now found only in Mongolia. There, they are called takhi, meaning "spirit."** • Horses

like sweet flavors. • **Mares carry their babies for about a year before giving birth.** • Horse teeth never stop growing. • **Just like humans, horses start with a set of baby teeth, also known as milk teeth.** • A young horse's milk teeth are all replaced with adult teeth by about age five. • **Under a horse's hoof, there is an area called the "frog" that acts as a natural shock absorber.** • The record for the highest jump by a horse was more than 8 feet (2.4 m). • **It takes about a year for a horse to regrow a new hoof.** • A zony is

HORSES ARE SOCIAL—THEY LIKE TO BE AROUND OTHER HORSES.

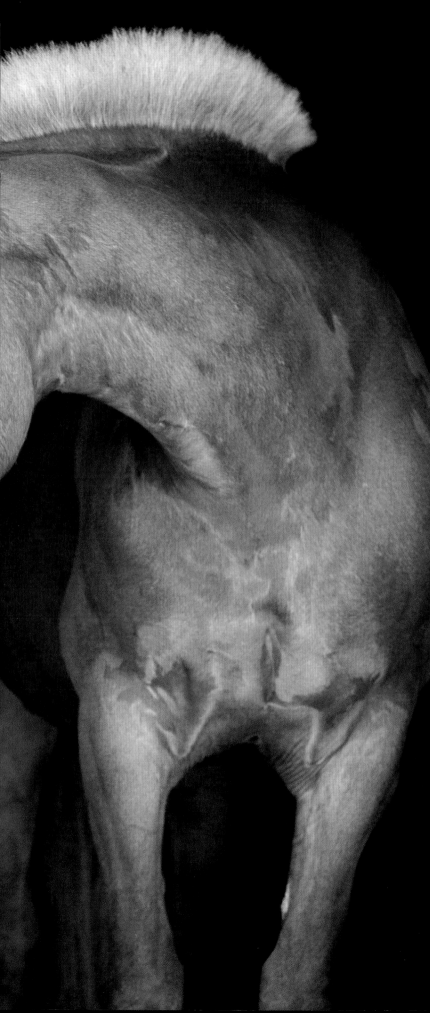

Horses Sleep Standing Up!

HORSES HAVE THE ABILITY TO SLEEP WHILE STANDING. Considering how large the average horse is, it can take a lot of effort and time for a horse to hoist its big body up from the ground. Instead, horses can snooze thanks to a mechanism in their bodies called the "stay apparatus." This system of tendons and ligaments **acts like a built-in hammock,** locking the major leg joints into place so the horse can completely relax its muscles without falling over. Even when they're not dozing, sometimes horses rest in this position. **For deep sleep, horses do need to lie down.** Compared with other animals such as lions that sleep up to 20 hours a day, horses don't need much sleep. **With just two or three hours of deep sleep, a horse is ready to go.**

a cross between a zebra and a pony. • **A Thoroughbred racing horse named Fusaichi Pegasus sold for more than $60 million.** • The 3-million-year-old Hagerman horse fossils discovered in Idaho, U.S.A., in 1928 are the earliest known evidence of modern horses. • **Mules are the offspring of a male donkey and a female horse.** • A hinny mule is the offspring of a horse father and donkey mother. • **Feral horses are those that escaped from groups of domesticated horses and now roam free.** • Assateague Island, Maryland, U.S.A., is home to feral ponies that can be seen running along its beaches. • **A horse's heart is about 13 times larger than the heart of an adult male human.** • Foals stop drinking from their mothers at between four and eight months old. At that point, they care called weanlings.

A guide horse at work

Spectacularly

AN ARTHROPOD IS AN
INVERTEBRATE THAT
HAS MANY LEGS.

Spineless

Centipede

50 Totally Random Facts About INVERTEBRATES

Some invertebrates have a skeleton on the outside of their bodies; others have internal skeletons. • Insects, spiders, and lobsters are all arthropods. • **Arthropods make up 84 percent of all known animal species on the planet.** • There are 10,000 species of sponges. • **If a worm is cut in half, the part with the "head" sometimes grows a new tail.** • A kind of millipede in central California, U.S.A., has 750 legs. • **The colossal squid is the world's largest invertebrate. It can** grow over 40 feet (12 m) long, weigh half a ton (454 kg), and sport eyes the size of melons. • The longest invertebrate in the world is the ribbon worm, which can stretch 180 feet (55 m). • **Horseshoe crabs have blue blood.** • There are about 100,000 kinds of mollusk, making up nearly a fourth of all marine organisms. • **Some invertebrates do not have heads.** • The world's smallest invertebrate—the wheel animal—can be as small as a credit card is thick. You need a microscope to see one. • **Lobsters, crabs, and shrimp all have 10 legs.** • When crustaceans outgrow their shells, they shed them and grow a new one. • **Centipedes are carnivores that eat insects.** • Millipedes are herbivores that eat plants. • **There are about 2,700 kinds of earthworm.** • In 1 acre (0.4 ha) of land, there can be more than a million earthworms. • **An earthworm's front end can sense light even though it doesn't have eyes.** • Known as living fossils, horseshoe crabs date back 450 million years. • **Most invertebrates go through**

A horseshoe crab lying upside down. Horseshoe crabs have six pairs of legs.

Red fire millipede

European stag beetles only live a few weeks after becoming adults.

Blue moth fly

There are millions of invertebrates living in your house right now. They are known as **DUST MITES.**

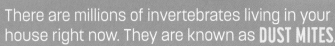
Red sea star

a metamorphosis, or change in form. • Horseshoe crabs are more closely related to spiders and ticks than crabs. • **Sea stars have hundreds of tiny feet.** • Scientists use horseshoe crab blood to test new aedicines. • **Some invertebrates, like corals and bees, form large colonies that live like one huge organism.** • Jellyfish don't have hearts or brains. • **Scientists think the first invertebrates existed 600 million to a billion years ago.** •

Octopuses and squid can change their colors to hide from predators. • **Though most sponges can't move by themselves, some can move very slowly.** • Most parasites, which live in or on another organism, are invertebrates. • **Earthworms have no arms, legs, or eyes.** • Scientists study invertebrates to learn about genetics. • **Most invertebrates lay eggs.** • Earthworms breathe through their skin. • **Mites are the fastest animals in the world relative**

THAT'S SO RANDOM:

Invertebrates Hold the World Record for Most Species!

INVERTEBRATES ARE ANIMALS THAT DON'T HAVE A BACKBONE OR A BONY SKELETON. About 97 percent of the world's animal species are invertebrates. That makes them the largest group of animals on Earth! The other 3 percent includes the rest of Earth's animals—all the mammals, fish, reptiles, and birds combined. **More than 1.25 million different species of invertebrates are known to exist, and scientists think a lot more are waiting to be discovered.** These mighty creatures come in many shapes and sizes. Sea stars, sea cucumbers, and sea urchins are in a group called echinoderms. **Cnidarians include jellyfish, corals, and sea anemones. Snails, slugs, squid, and octopuses make up the mollusk group.** Then you have poriferans, which include sponges; annelids, which include worms; and arthropods, which include insects, spiders, and lobsters. Arthropods have jointed legs and exoskeletons. **There are more than 800,000 arthropod species, the most of any group of invertebrates.**

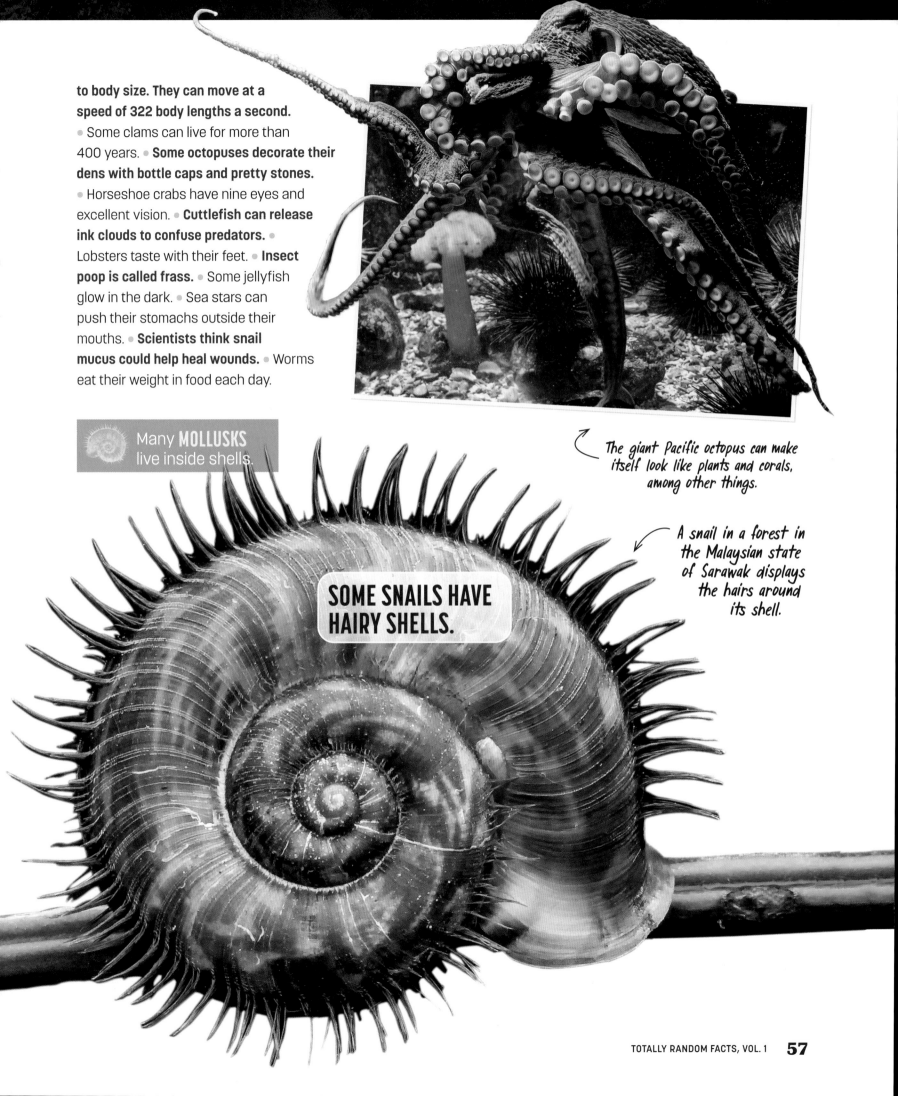

to body size. They can move at a speed of 322 body lengths a second. • Some clams can live for more than 400 years. • **Some octopuses decorate their dens with bottle caps and pretty stones.** • Horseshoe crabs have nine eyes and excellent vision. • **Cuttlefish can release ink clouds to confuse predators.** • Lobsters taste with their feet. • **Insect poop is called frass.** • Some jellyfish glow in the dark. • Sea stars can push their stomachs outside their mouths. • **Scientists think snail mucus could help heal wounds.** • Worms eat their weight in food each day.

Many **MOLLUSKS** live inside shells.

The giant Pacific octopus can make itself look like plants and corals, among other things.

SOME SNAILS HAVE HAIRY SHELLS.

A snail in a forest in the Malaysian state of Sarawak displays the hairs around its shell.

A polar bear hunting a beluga whale

Beluga whale

There are eight bear species: giant panda, brown bear, North American black bear, polar bear, sloth bear, spectacled bear, sun bear, and Asiatic black bear. • **"Grizzly bear" is a common name given to a subspecies of the North American brown bear.** • Bears are found in North and South America, Europe, and Asia. • **Spectacled bears build platforms in trees to help them reach fruit hanging near the top.** • Fewer than 2,000 giant pandas live in the wild. • **The sun bear is the smallest bear species, weighing between 60 and 150 pounds (27 and 68 kg).** • Giant pandas communicate by barking, chirping, honking, and bleating. • **Scientists think the distinct black-and-white coat of the giant panda might help pandas camouflage in the wild.** • Each spectacled bear's cream-colored markings

Spirit bear

are unique, just like fingerprints. • **Rare white bears, known as spirit bears, live on just a few islands along the coast of British Columbia, Canada. Scientists believe only about 100 exist.** • Giant pandas are native to forests in the mountains of central China. • **Spectacled bears mostly live alone.** • Finding food and eating takes up 10 to 16 hours of a giant panda's day. • **Of all bear species, only the brown bear and North American black bear populations are not considered threatened or vulnerable to extinction.** • Giant pandas need to eat a lot of bamboo to get the nutrients they need—20 to 80 pounds (9–36 kg) a day. • **Spirit bears are actually black bears that have white fur.** • Bamboo makes up about 99 percent of a panda's diet. • **Polar bears have black skin.** • Asiatic black bears are also called "moon bears" due to the white or cream-colored, crescent-shaped mark on their chests. • **Male**

Bear Necessities

50 Totally Random Facts About PANDAS and OTHER BEARS

SUN BEARS USE THEIR 10-INCH (25 CM) TONGUES TO SLURP UP THE INSECTS THEY EAT.

Panda Babies

- A newborn panda cub weighs about as much as a stick of butter.
- **Panda cubs are born pink, hairless, and tiny. At birth they're 1/900 the size of their mothers.**
- A panda cub will stay with its mother for about 18 months.
- **Female pandas can have twins, but they usually only have one baby at a time.**

pandas sometimes do handstands. • Pandas are vulnerable to becoming extinct, but conservation programs are helping save the species. • **Polar bears, the largest bears in the world, can weigh 1,600 pounds (725 kg).** • Giant pandas are solitary animals. • **In winters when food is hard** to find, some bears survive by hibernating, or resting to save energy. • American black bears can go up to 100 days without drinking or eating while in hibernation. • **Bear cubs are born blind.** • Polar bear fur is transparent and the hairs are hollow. • **Giant pandas do not hibernate.** • Female bears that hibernate wake up and give birth to up to four cubs. • **Winnie the Pooh isn't the only bear to love honey—all bears like the sweet, sticky goo.** • Sloth bears are speedy eaters, slurping up termites at record speed. • **Sun bears live in the tropical forests and swamps of Southeast Asia.** • When a polar bear and a grizzly bear mate, their cub is called a "pizzly bear." • **Spectacled bears are the only bears native to South America.** • Sloth bears can completely close their nostrils, keeping insects out of their noses when they eat. • **Giant pandas live about 15 to 20 years in the wild.** • A polar bear is successful on a hunt only about 2 percent of the time. • **Pandas have wide, flat molar teeth that help chomp and grind bamboo stalks.** • Polar bears are very smart. They can complete complex tasks with multiple steps. • **Before hibernating, black bears eat so much that they gain about 30 pounds (14 kg) a week.** • About 600 giant pandas live in zoos around the world. • **Polar bears sometimes slide down ice hills for fun.** • Spectacled bears are primarily nocturnal. • **A sun bear's curved claws help it move from tree to tree. These bears are also nocturnal.**

GIANT PANDAS POOP EVEN WHEN THEY ARE SLEEPING.

Crafty Canines

Baby foxes are called kits or pups.

A female fox is called a vixen.

Foxes are members of the Canidae family, just like dogs and wolves.

Like cats, foxes have spines on their tongue.

To protect them from the hot sand they walk on, fennec foxes have fur on their feet.

43 Totally Random Facts About FOXES

Red foxes can hear prey, such as rodents, digging underground.

A thick fur coat helps keep red foxes warm in the winter.

Red foxes don't always notice an animal or object that's still, but they can quickly see things that are moving.

In addition to their great hearing, red foxes depend of their excellent sense of smell to find prey.

In addition to small animals such as rabbits, red foxes also eat plants and berries.

Arctic foxes can detect prey under the snow. They listen for their meal, then dive in to catch it!

The scientific name for the bat-eared fox means "dog with big ears" in Greek.

Arctic fox

Gray foxes can climb trees.

Bat-eared foxes live in savannas in eastern and southern Africa. Termites and other insects make up most of their diet.

Female red foxes have anywhere from 1 to 12 pups in a single litter.

Bengal foxes live in the foothills of the Himalaya Mountains and in northern India.

Red foxes have fluffy, white-tipped tails.

Foxes have whiskers on their legs to help them find their way through tall grasses.

Both bat-eared foxes and fennec foxes use their huge ears to listen for and detect prey underground.

Fantastic Fennecs

- **Fennec foxes are the smallest fox species in the world.**

- Fennec foxes live in the Sahara and other desert regions of North Africa, as well as the Sinai and Arabian Peninsulas.

- **At 4 to 6 inches (10–15 cm) long, a fennec fox's large ears help the fox release body heat to stay cool in its desert home.**

- Fennec foxes can jump 2 to 3 feet (0.6–1 m) into the air.

Red foxes can be found anywhere from forests and farmlands to suburban neighborhoods.

The island fox lives only on the Channel Islands off the coast of California.

A group of foxes is called a skulk or a leash.

Foxes are mostly nocturnal—or active at night—and stay in their dens during the day.

Foxes bark, chatter, and howl to communicate.

Foxes use their tails to signal to other foxes.

Unlike other members of the canid family, which includes dogs, wolves, coyotes, and foxes, gray foxes have retractable claws, similar to cats.

Arctic foxes live in the Far North where temperatures get frigid. They use their fluffy tails as a blanket to keep warm.

Foxes make underground dens that usually have more than one exit.

Swift foxes live in deserts and prairies.

Crab-eating foxes are native to South America. They live in grasslands, woodlands, and forests.

The crab-eating fox gets its name from the prey it eats. In the rainy season where the fox lives, crabs show up on muddy floodplains, making the perfect snack.

FOXES ARE BORN DEAF, TOOTHLESS, AND BLIND. IT TAKES ABOUT 9 TO 14 DAYS FOR THEIR EYES TO OPEN.

Small rodents called lemmings are an arctic fox's favorite food.

In winter the arctic fox's snowy white coat helps it blend in with its surroundings.

Bat-eared foxes have up to 50 teeth. That's more than most other mammals.

The swift fox, the smallest fox in North America, is about the size of a house cat.

Bengal foxes have long, bushy tails that make up more than half the length of their bodies.

Hoary foxes live in the grasslands of southwestern Brazil in South America. They are gray with reddish legs and ears.

Arctic foxes don't hibernate, but in extreme cold they will stay in their dens and slow their heart rates to save energy.

Rainbow Reptiles

41 Totally Random Facts About CHAMELEONS

Chameleons eat insects such as crickets and mealworms.

Chameleons that live in trees are usually green.

Chameleons that live in deserts are usually brown.

When a chameleon turns darker, it may be trying to warm itself up. When it turns light green, it may be trying to cool off.

When a chameleon turns bright colors, it is likely either to attract a mate or to threaten an enemy.

A chameleon's eyes can move in two directions at once, letting the reptile see 360 degrees around.

Many chameleon species have a small set of horns on their heads. Males use them to fight.

Chameleons live mostly in rain forests and deserts of Africa.

There are more than 150 species of chameleons.

About two-thirds of chameleon species live only on the African island of Madagascar.

The world's smallest chameleon, the _Brookesia nana_, is about the size of a sunflower seed.

The largest chameleon is the Parson's chameleon, which can reach a length of 27 inches (68 cm), or the size of a house cat.

A chameleon's tongue is about twice the length of its body.

Chameleons don't stop growing.

Chameleons are related to iguanas.

Chameleon tongues can move from 0 to 60 miles an hour (96 kmh) in a hundredth of a second to snatch prey.

Meller's chameleons can live up to 12 years in the wild.

Some species of chameleon, including the tiger chameleon, the Belalanda chameleon, and the bizarre-nosed chameleon, are endangered.

The female Jackson's chameleon gives birth to 8 to 30 babies at a time.

Like snakes, chameleons do not have ears. Instead, chameleons hear by detecting sound through a membrane in their head.

Since chameleons have such broad eye movement, they can look at two different objects at the same time, or they can focus on one object with both eyes.

Baby chameleons are called hatchlings.

Some species of chameleon give birth to live young, but most lay eggs.

Most chameleons have prehensile, or grasping, tails that wrap around tree branches as the animal climbs.

Chameleons drink water by licking dew off leaves.

Veiled chameleons, which live in mountain areas with little water, have a special growth on their heads called a casque. It acts as a funnel to capture water that drips into the chameleon's mouth.

Larger chameleons eat small birds and lizards.

To pull prey into their mouths, chameleons use a small ball of muscle at the end of their tongue that sticks to prey like a suction cup.

Each species of chameleon has a specific group of patterns that it can display.

Chameleon hatchlings can hunt insects within a few days of being born.

Chameleon spit is 400 times stickier than human spit. This helps them snatch prey.

Male and female chameleons have different coloring.

Chameleons have tong-like feet that help them grasp tree branches.

Chameleons are not social and prefer to live alone.

Some chameleon eggs take more than a year to hatch.

The Skinny on Skin

- The outer layer of a chameleon's skin is transparent, meaning you can see through it.

- **Chameleons have special cells under the outer layer of their skin that contain pigments that change color.**

- Chameleons have four layers of skin.

- **Chameleons change color by sending a message to their skin cells with their brain. The cells release pigment that makes a new skin tone, kind of like mixing paint.**

- Chameleons shed their skin a little at a time.

Panther chameleon

Unlike many other types of lizards, if a chameleon's tail breaks off, **IT CAN'T REGROW.**

Din-o-mite!

95 Totally Random Facts About DINOSAURS

Dinosaurs roamed Earth for about 170 to 180 million years. • The name Dinosauria is derived from the Greek *deinos*, meaning "fearfully great," and *sauros*, meaning "lizard." • **Dinosaur fossils have been discovered on all seven continents, even Antarctica.** • Sixty-six million years ago, all dinosaurs that couldn't fly disappeared from the planet. • **Paleontologists are scientists who study animals that went extinct, including dinosaurs.** • *Ankylosaurus* was a plant-eating dinosaur that had leaf-shaped teeth used for grinding the plants it ate. • **Paleontologists have discovered and named about 1,000 species of dinosaurs.** • Teeth, bone, shell, egg, and even dung fossils give us important clues about how dinosaurs lived. • **Fossils are the only proof that dinosaurs existed.** • Paleontologists think that some dinosaur species traveled in packs with adults and young. • **Dinosaurs first appeared on Earth during the Triassic period, approximately 250 to 200 million years ago.** • All dinosaurs did not live together at the same time. For example, when *T. rex* lived, *Stegosaurus* had been extinct for about 70 million years. • **During the Triassic period, Earth was one piece of land called Pangaea.** • In the Jurassic period, about 199 to 145 million years ago, Earth's

Diplodocus used its long neck to reach for leaves high in trees.

Pteranodons were flying reptiles. They lived from about 90 to 100 million years ago.

land was split into two separate continents. • **Scientists believe that an asteroid the size of a mountain struck Earth, leading to the mass extinction that killed off most dinosaurs.** • The Cretaceous period was the last era when dinosaurs lived on Earth. It was 145 to 66 million years ago. • **During the Cretaceous period, Earth's continents were in almost the same areas as they are now.** • *Iguanodon* had a unique

SCIENTISTS ARE NOT SURE IF DINOSAURS WERE WARM-BLOODED LIKE BIRDS, COLD-BLOODED LIKE REPTILES, OR A COMBINATION OF BOTH.

thumb spike on each of its hands. When the dinosaur was first discovered, the thumb spike was mistaken for a horn. • **Trackways are fossils of footprints that give paleontologists information on how dinosaurs moved.** •

T. rex was a carnivore with curved, sharp teeth that gulped chunks of food whole instead of chewing first. • **Plant-eating dinosaurs, such as *Triceratops*, had hundreds of teeth in tight rows that they used to chop off branches.** • *Diplodocus* was a long-necked dinosaur that would use its long, skinny teeth to rake leaves off trees. • **Some dinosaurs ate rocks to help grind up their food. Birds such as parakeets and chickens do this, too.** • Paleontologists can estimate a dinosaur's height up to its hip from the size of its footprint. • **Fossilized footprints that show three toes and sharp claws were likely made by a carnivore, or meat-eater.** • *Triceratops* was about 30 feet (9 m) long, and its frilled head was HUGE—roughly a third the size of its entire body. • **Scientists have found areas in the United States and Brazil that might be locations where dinosaurs peed.** • Millions of fossilized dinosaur footprints have been found in Colorado, U.S.A., leading paleontologists to believe that some dinosaurs migrated. • *Psittacosaurus* (sih-TACK-oh-sore-us) translates to "parrot lizard." A very

Triceratops skull

Tyrannosaurus rex was a top predator when it roamed Earth 68 million years ago.

Triceratops might have used its horns to fight predators, including T. rex.

fitting name for a dinosaur that had a parrotlike beak. • Today's birds have nearly identical skeletal features to some non-avian dinosaurs. • **The heaviest dinosaur of all time was *Argentinosaurus*. It weighed 99 to 110 tons (90–100 metric tons) and was about 121 to 131 feet (37–40 m) long.** • Dinosaur National Monument on the border of Colorado and Utah is home to a sandstone wall containing about 1,500 fossils of dinosaur bones. • **All dinosaurs lived on land.** • Dinosaurs had a unique physical trait: a hole in their hip socket that allowed them to stand upright. • **A total population about 2.5 billion *T. rexes* once roamed Earth.** • Some dinosaurs made nests to lay their eggs. • **A quick and vicious killer, *Deinonychus* had a retractable claw.** • Some large dinosaurs, including *Apatosaurus*, lived for 70 to 80 years, which is about the life span

Ankylosaurus

of an elephant. • **Some dinosaurs had skulls with holes in them, which helped keep their brains cool.** • The first dinosaur ever named was *Megalosaurus*, in 1824. • **The first dinosaur fossil was discovered in 1677. Back then, dinosaurs were unknown and people thought it belonged to a giant human.** • The average dinosaur was about the size of a car. • **A nearly complete *T. rex* skeleton sold at auction for $31.8 million, breaking the record for the highest price paid for dinosaur fossils.** • The biggest dinosaur eggs ever discovered belong to *Segnosaurus*. They were about 19 inches (48 cm) long and looked like a deflated football. • **The smallest dinosaur egg fossil ever found is smaller than a golf ball. It was**

discovered in Japan in 2020. • The dinosaur with the longest name is *Micropachycephalosaurus*, which means "tiny, thick-headed lizard." It's also one of the smallest dinosaurs. • **Until the first-known dinosaur eggs in Mongolia's Gobi desert were discovered in 1923, scientists didn't know how dinosaurs reproduced.** • *Tyrannosaurus* had the longest teeth of any carnivorous dinosaur. At 8 inches (20 cm), they were about the length of a banana, but super sharp. • **The largest dinosaurs were plant-eaters.** • Of all the meat-eating dinosaurs ever discovered, the smallest was the size of a blue jay. • **The strongest dinosaur was likely *Ultrasaurus*, a beast as big as a six-story building.** • The oldest known dino was *Eoraptor*, a dog-size carnivore that lived 228 million years ago. • **Torosaurus had an 8-foot (2.4-m)-long skull, which was bigger than any land animal.** • Dinosaurs usually walked on their toes. • *Ankylosaurus* had a built-in weapon: a large club at the end of its tail that it used to swipe at enemies. • Most large plant-eating dinosaurs had S-shaped necks. • *Pachycephalosaurus* had a very thick dome-shaped skull. It was up to 9 inches (23 cm) at the top. Its name means "thick-headed lizard." • One dinosaur is

SOME DINOSAURS EVOLVED FEATHERS TO KEEP THEM WARM AND TO ATTRACT MATES.

Scientists think Dakotaraptor was feathered but too large to fly.

Spinosaurus was the first dinosaur known to be a swimmer.

Earth being hit by an asteroid

named after Harry Potter's school: *Dracorex hogwartsia*. • **The largest dinosaur eggs could hold about a gallon (3.7 L) of milk.** • The duck-billed Parasaurolophus made a trumpetlike sound. • *Epidendrosaurus* **had an extra-long third finger on each hand, was about the size of a sparrow, and is believed to have lived in trees.** • The largest and most complete *T. rex* ever discovered is nicknamed Sue, and she lives at the Field Museum in Chicago, Illinois, U.S.A. • **Scientists can determine what time of day a dinosaur was most active by looking at the shape of the eye sockets in fossils.** • *T. rex* could see 13 times better than humans. • **You could easily climb through *T. rex*'s jaw, because it was 4 feet (1.2 m) long**. • *Stegosaurus* had quite a small brain for such a large dinosaur. Paleontologists have described the brain as being the shape of a bent hot dog and about the same size. • **More dinosaurs have been discovered in the United States than any other place in the world.** • *Ornithomimus* looked similar to an ostrich and had powerful legs and a beaked mouth. These dinosaurs were also fast runners. • **Some dinosaurs migrated hundreds of miles every year.** • When *Apatosaurus* whipped its long tail, scientists believe that the booming sound was so loud that it might have broken the sound barrier. • **Discovered in 1986, *Antarctopelta* was the first dinosaur found in Antarctica.** • *T. rex*'s brain was twice as big as the brains of the other huge meat-eating dinosaurs. • **Flying reptiles called pterosaurs were soaring through the skies at the same time** dinosaurs were roaming the land. • *Mamenchisaurus* had a 30-foot (9-m)-long neck, the longest of any animal in the world. • *Nigersaurus* **had more than 500 teeth, which would replace themselves every two weeks.** • Some dinosaurs got cancer, just like humans do. • **Scientists believe that dinosaurs were thriving on Earth before the asteroid that wiped them away hit our planet.** • Fossils of baby dinosaurs are very rare, so scientists know a lot more about adults. • *Spinosaurus* **had flat feet, dense bones, and a tail like a paddle, leading scientists to believe that it spent a lot of time in the water.** • *Titanosaurus* babies were born with a temporary rhino-like horn that helped them break out of their egg. • **The earliest dinosaur eggs were leathery and soft.** • Meat-eating dinosaurs laid long, thin eggs. Plant-eating dinosaurs laid eggs that were rounded. • *Asteriornis*, **called the "wonderchicken" by scientists, is the oldest-known ancestor of modern birds.** • Some dinosaurs stayed in polar habitats year-round. • **Reptiles were also in the oceans during the time of dinosaurs. A fossil of *Mosasaurus*, a fierce marine reptile, showed that it was 56 feet (17 m) long.** • Experts believe *Baryonyx* was an expert fisher: Fish scales were found with its fossil. • **Not all dinosaurs were discovered by paleontologists. *Mamenchisaurus* was found by builders working on a bridge in China.** • *Conchoraptor* was a small, toothless dinosaur, but it had a very powerful beak, likely used to crack open shelled prey such as crabs.

Dinosaurs Are Related to Chickens!

YOU MIGHT BE SURPRISED TO LEARN THAT THE CLOSEST LIVING RELATIVES OF *TYRANNOSAURUS REX* ARE BIRDS SUCH AS OSTRICHES AND CHICKENS. The link between feathered friends and dinosaurs has been suspected for many years based on similarities that both animals have. Then, one dino bone helped strengthen that theory. **Paleontologists found a giant dinosaur femur while digging in a remote Montana, U.S.A., field.** To fit the giant bone into the helicopter to transfer it to the lab, they had to break it in half. In the lab, scientists were able to retrieve from inside the bone molecules of collagen, a protein that gives structure and appears in slightly different forms in many animals. **Obtaining actual molecules of an animal that lived 65 million years ago was the key for unlocking the connection.** Using this new molecular evidence, they compared the dinosaur version with 21 living animals, including humans, chimps, mice, chickens, ostriches, alligators, and salmon. ***T. rex*'s collagen proved to be most similar to that of chickens and ostriches; its next closest match was to alligators.** Chickens and ostriches are not closely related, even though they are both birds. To learn the *T. rex*'s closest avian kin, paleontologists would need access to the dinosaur's DNA, which they don't have, yet.

Aquatic Avians

74 Totally Random Facts About PENGUINS

There are 18 species of penguin.

Penguins are seabirds that mostly live below the equator.

The only species to live outside the Southern Hemisphere is the Galápagos penguin.

Penguins only lay one or two eggs at a time.

Most birds have hollow bones, but penguins' bones are solid, which helps them swim.

Penguins are among the few birds that cannot fly.

Most penguins swim 4 to 7 miles an hour (6.5 to 11 kmh).

Penguins spend up to 80 percent of their lives at sea.

IN THE WATER, A GROUP OF PENGUINS IS CALLED A RAFT.

Tuxedos are nicknamed penguin suits because all penguins have black bodies and white bellies.

A penguin's white belly blends in with the ocean's surface as it swims, helping it hide from predators below.

Sharks, sea lions, whales, and leopard seals prey on penguins.

Penguins live in groups called colonies.

Colonies can have thousands or even millions of members living together.

To stay warm and defend against predators, penguins huddle together.

Penguins can weigh between 2 and 88 pounds (1 and 40 kg).

Emperor penguins

Gentoo penguin

little blue penguin

Gentoo penguins are the speediest swimmers, gliding up to 22 miles an hour (35 kmh).

Penguins "toboggan" by sliding on their bellies to travel long distances.

True to their name, rockhopper penguins hop from rock to rock rather than waddle like other penguins.

Penguins lay eggs on land, or on pack ice.

Penguin parents have a unique call for their chicks, so they can find them in a crowd.

Penguins produce their own waterproof oil, which they use to cover their feathers to help them glide through water as they swim.

All of a penguin's feathers are shed at once, a process known as a catastrophic molt.

Catastrophic molts take place once a year and last for two to three weeks.

When penguins are molting, they can't hunt for food because they're not waterproof.

Polar bears and penguins are not neighbors. Penguins live south of the equator, whereas polar bears live north of the equator in the Arctic.

Some species of penguin trek 60 miles (97 km) to their breeding grounds.

The longest recorded penguin dive is 22 minutes.

Streamlined, torpedo-shaped bodies help penguins zoom through the water.

The little blue penguin weighs less than 3 pounds (1.4 kg), making it the smallest penguin species.

Penguins live for about 15 to 20 years.

In Australia, little blue penguins are called fairy penguins because of their small size—just over a foot (30 cm) tall.

Some penguins can launch 6 to 9 feet (1.8–2.7 m) into the air as they burst out of the water to get to floating sea ice.

CHINSTRAP PENGUINS are the most plentiful kind of penguin.

Many male penguins give females rocks as gifts. The females use them to build nests.

Male Adélie penguins build nests out of rocks to impress females. Sometimes they steal rocks from each other.

The smallest penguins in the Antarctic, Adélies are feisty and will defend themselves against seals and seabirds.

Penguins have a special gland above their eyes that helps them remove excess salt from their bodies.

Penguins use their wings like flippers to propel themselves through water.

Before leaping from the water to the ice, penguins release air bubbles from their feathers to boost their speed.

Penguins don't have teeth. Instead, spiny flesh in their mouths and throats helps them swallow fish whole.

Hoiho penguins have yellow eyes. They are found on islands off the coast of New Zealand.

Adélie and emperor penguins are the only two penguin species that live solely in Antarctica.

The earliest known penguin fossils date back 62 million years.

King penguins (adults and chicks)

King penguin chick

Penguins have special vision that lets them see underwater as well as they can on land.

More than 37 million years ago, a giant penguin weighed 200 pounds (91 kg) and stood nearly 6 feet (1.8 m) tall!

Penguin feathers are waterproof and windproof.

The New Zealand giant, a supersized penguin ancestor from 30 million years ago, weighed about 130 pounds (59 kg) and stood 5 feet (1.5 m) tall.

ROCKHOPPERS have red eyes, pink feet, an orange beak, and yellow feathers sprouting from their heads.

ON LAND, A GROUP OF PENGUINS IS CALLED A WADDLE.

Emperor penguins on the march

Small penguins mostly feed at the surface of the water, slurping up krill and squid.

In all penguin species except the emperor penguin, both the mother and father penguin take turns caring for their eggs.

The little blue penguin lays the smallest eggs. They're only 2 ounces (57 g), which is about the weight of a half-stick of butter.

Penguins are carnivores. They eat fish, krill, and other food they catch in the water.

In the Antarctic, adult penguins have no predators on land.

Skuas, a type of gull, prey on penguin eggs and hatchlings.

African penguins have up to 70 feathers per square inch (6.5 sq cm).

Penguin feathers are stiff and overlap in layers. This helps the feathers trap a pocket of air that acts as insulation to keep the birds warm and dry.

Gentoos, rockhoppers, and chinstraps are monogamous. Some stick with one partner for the season, others stay with the same partner for life.

Using unique sounds, Adélie females can locate their old mates as soon as they reach their breeding grounds.

Large penguin colonies are called rookeries. Rookeries can have hundreds of thousands of members.

Penguins are one of the most endangered seabirds. About two-thirds of penguins are listed as threatened.

Climate change has a direct effect on penguins because they live on the sea ice of Antarctica, the melting of which is due to rising temperatures.

Snares penguins, found in New Zealand, build their nests in forests.

The yellow feathers on the macaroni penguin's head look like the ones in the 18th-century hats noted in the song "Yankee Doodle."

Humboldt penguins blush to prevent overheating.

Penguins can drink seawater.

Emperors of the Ice

- The emperor penguin is the only bird species to nest in the Antarctic during winter.

- Emperor penguins are the largest penguin species, reaching up to 47 inches (120 cm) tall. This is about the height of a six-year-old kid.

- The deepest diver of all species is the emperor penguin, which can dive up to 1,850 feet (564 m) below the surface.

- Emperor penguins keep their eggs warm on their feet. Males put them under a special fold of skin, which acts like a blanket.

- Male emperor penguins care for their eggs alone for two to three months while the female goes to hunt. During this time, males can lose half their body weight.

- Emperor penguins lay the largest eggs, which weigh about 1 pound (0.5 kg), the same as four sticks of butter.

- Emperor penguins have at least four different kinds of feathers that help them stay warm in the icy water.

Here, Kitty, Kitty

49 Totally Random Facts About *CATS*

The bond between humans and felines dates back about 12,000 years to the Middle East.

There are about 500 million pet cats around the globe today.

Cats walk like camels and giraffes, using both right feet and then both left feet.

The first cat to go up in space, in 1963, survived the journey.

A statue in Scotland is dedicated to a cat that caught 30,000 mice.

Scientists believe that cats treat humans like very large cats.

JUST LIKE SOME HUMANS, SOME CATS ARE AMBIDEXTROUS, WHICH MEANS THEY USE THEIR RIGHT AND LEFT PAWS EQUALLY.

A painted wildcat in the tomb of 12th Dynasty Egyptian noble Khnumhotep II at Beni Hasan in Upper Egypt

Cats have about 38 more bones than humans. (Humans have 206 bones, and cats, on average, have 244.)

Cats rest for up to 20 hours a day.

House cats are meat-munching carnivores.

Scientists believe that the ancient Egyptians probably tamed wild cats about 3,500 years ago to protect their grain from mice.

Not all sphinx cats are hairless. Some have soft fuzz covering their skin.

Cats can't taste sweets.

A cat's brain is about 2 inches (5 cm) long.

Male cats are more likely to be left-pawed, whereas females are more likely to be right-pawed.

A cat has an extra organ on the roof of its mouth to taste scents in the air.

Cats have unique noseprints, just like humans have unique fingerprints.

The average life span of an indoor cat is 10 to 15 years.

"Queen" is the word for a pregnant cat.

A young European spotted genet

A HOUSE CAT SHARES 95.6 PERCENT OF ITS GENES WITH A TIGER.

Cat brains have half the number of neurons of dog brains.

An older female cat is called a grimalkin.

While awake, cats spend a third of their time grooming.

Cats are crepuscular, which means they are most active during dawn and dusk. The middle of the day is mostly spent catnapping.

When a cat rubs its face against you, it's called bunting.

Cats can sprint at speeds of up to 30 miles an hour (48 kmh), but only for short bursts.

The term *caterwaul* comes from the wailing sound a cat makes when it looks for a mate.

When your cat sleeps belly up, it's a sign of trust.

Cats don't just groom to clean themselves—they also do it to relax.

Kneading, when a cat presses its paws gently into something, is a sign of happiness.

There are about 58 million pet cats in the United States.

Maine coons have three layers of fur. The two bottom layers repel water.

PEOPLE SPEND OVER A BILLION DOLLARS EVERY YEAR ON SERVICES AND ITEMS FOR THEIR KITTIES.

I ♥ My Cat

A cat's tongue has backward-facing hooks, that feel like sandpaper, **TO SCRAPE MEAT OFF BONES.**

A cat putting its rear end in your face is a sign of friendship.

Scientists believe that today's house cats descended from a Middle Eastern wildcat.

Cats don't meow at other cats.

Scientists discovered an ancient Egyptian cat cemetery with more than 300,000 cat mummies.

Ailurophobia is a fear of cats.

Cats sweat through their paws.

In 1983, archaeologists discovered an 8,000-year-old cat's jawbone.

Cats can dream.

Dogs were domesticated before cats, because they helped people hunt.

Cats can jump up to five times their own height.

For 20 years, a tabby cat named Stubbs was the mayor of a small Alaska town.

Creme Puff, the world's oldest cat, lived to be 38 years old.

A cat in Australia learned to ride and do tricks on a skateboard.

On the island of Key West in Florida, U.S.A., many of the cats have an extra toe.

All kittens are born with blue eyes.

A gray-and-white tabby cat relaxes with its belly up, a sign of trust.

Cats' Purrfect Habit!

CATS DON'T PURR ON PURPOSE, THEY DO IT BY INSTINCT. Purring is a continuous sound made by the muscles in a cat's throat and chest as a cat breathes. **Cats purr to communicate with those close to them.** Why do they purr? One theory: The sound of a mother's purr helps quiet the cries of her nursing kittens, a sound that might otherwise alert and attract predators. Mostly cats purr when they are happy and content, like when they are nursing, grooming, relaxing, or being friendly. But not always. **Sometimes cats purr to signal when they are scared, hungry, or hurt.** In these cases, cats are purring to self-soothe. In fact, purring may have healing properties. The vibrations from a cat's purr promote tissue and bone growth. **Since cats spend a lot of time lying around, purring may keep their bones strong so they're ready to hunt for that mouse in the house.**

Life at the Top

56 Totally Random Facts About GIRAFFES

A giraffe's tongue is about 18 inches (46 cm) long!

The giraffe is the tallest land animal in the world.

Giraffes can run up to 35 miles an hour (56 kmh) in short bursts.

Giraffes only drink water once every few days.

A giraffe's body can adjust its blood flow to protect itself from fainting as it lowers and lifts its head to drink.

NASA has studied giraffes' legs to get ideas for building better human space suits.

A giraffe's heart is the biggest of any land mammal, weighing in at about 25 pounds (11 kg).

A giraffe's heart pumps 15.8 gallons (60 L) of blood around its body every minute.

There are about 117,000 giraffes in the wild in Africa.

People once called giraffes "camel leopards" because they look like a combination of the two animals.

Giraffes are herbivores, or plant-eaters, eating mainly leaves and buds on trees and shrubs.

A group of giraffes is called a tower.

There are four different kinds of giraffes: northern, southern, reticulated, and Masai.

Most giraffes live in grasslands and woodlands throughout Africa.

Giraffe tongues are a bluish-purple color.

Giraffe feet are the size of dinner plates.

Both male and female giraffes have "horns" on their heads called ossicones.

Giraffes bellow, snort, hiss, hum, and make flutelike sounds.

Female giraffes are called cows.

Giraffes go to watering holes in groups so they can take turns watching for predators.

To drink, a giraffe reaches the surface of the water by spreading its forelegs and bending its knees.

Lions and leopards are a giraffe's main predators. But it's not common for adult giraffes to fall prey to predators.

When it comes to food, a giraffe's height is a major advantage, allowing the animal to pluck leaves off branches that are too high for other animals to reach.

Giraffes often rest while standing upright.

Giraffes can spot movement from more than half a mile (0.8 km) away.

Giraffe mothers will protect their young by delivering a powerful kick to any other animal that comes too close.

Male giraffes will often leave their mothers at about 15 months old to join a group of other young males.

Scientists think giraffes sleep for several hours a day. Some of that time they sleep standing up.

People around the globe celebrate World Giraffe Day on June 21—the longest day or night of the year (depending on your hemisphere) to celebrate the tallest animal.

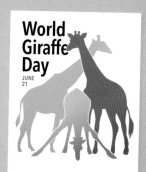

Young female giraffes usually live in the same herd as their mothers.

Giraffes can live for about 25 years in captivity. Little is known about how old they can get in the wild, but probably about the same, if not older.

Adult male giraffes are called bulls.

For very short periods of time, giraffes can sleep with their head resting on their rump.

EVERY GIRAFFE HAS A UNIQUE COAT PATTERN, KIND OF LIKE A HUMAN FINGERPRINT.

GIRAFFES HAVE EYES THE SIZE OF GOLF BALLS.

Giraffe Manor, Kenya

A herd of giraffes live on the property of a hotel called Giraffe Manor in Nairobi, Kenya, where the animals often poke their heads in through the windows.

At certain times of the year, a giraffe can spend up to 75 percent of its day eating.

Giraffes have prehensile lips, which means their lips can grasp things such as the leaves they eat.

When giraffes aren't eating, they're often seen chewing their cud—the ball of leaves that travels back up their throat after they swallow.

The okapi, the giraffe's closest relative, has a similar body shape but is smaller with a much shorter neck.

Okapi

The patches on a giraffe's fur help camouflage it.

Scientists think the dark color of a giraffe's tongue could help protect it from sunburns.

An adult male giraffe can grow to be 18 feet (5.5 m) tall—about the height of a two-story building.

Giraffes can eat up to 75 pounds (34 kg) of food in a single day.

A giraffe's thick, sticky saliva coats the thorns from the acacia trees they eat, so the giraffes can swallow them without getting hurt.

Male giraffes fight each other using their necks. This is called necking.

Beneath each patch on a giraffe's coat is a system of blood vessels, allowing each patch to release body heat.

Giraffes fold their legs under their bodies when they lie down.

Giraffes get a lot of the water they need from the acacia leaves that they eat.

GIRAFFES HAVE SEVEN VERTEBRAE IN THEIR NECKS, AND SO DO HUMANS.

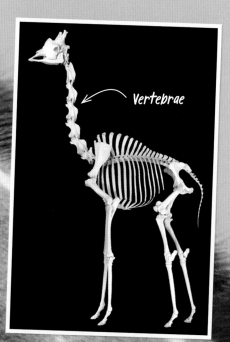

Vertebrae

BIG BABY!

- **Mother giraffes carry their babies for about 15 months before they are born.**

- **Female giraffes give birth standing up. The babies fall about 6 feet (2 m) to the ground.**

- **Newborn giraffes are taller than most humans.**

- **Baby giraffes can stand up within an hour of being born.**

- **Newborn giraffes can nearly double their height within their first year of life.**

- **Usually, a giraffe will only have one calf, but twins have been recorded.**

SLOTHS SPEND MOST OF THEIR LIVES UPSIDE DOWN.

A baby three-toed sloth

Slow Motion

45 Totally Random Facts About SLOTHS

Sloths are related to armadillos and anteaters. • **Sloths only go to the bathroom once a week.** • In the wild, sloths sleep for about 8 to 10 hours a day. • **Sloths don't have much muscle, so they can't shiver to warm up when they feel cold.** • The Spanish word for sloths is *los perezosos*, meaning "the lazies." • **Sloths move slowly, which helps them avoid the attention of predators.** • The sloth is the slowest mammal on Earth. • **Sloths move an average of about 120 feet** (37 m) per day. • The pygmy three-toed sloth is the smallest sloth on Earth. It is found only on a small island off the coast of Panama. • **Sloths are so slow that algae have enough time to grow on their fur, providing both extra camouflage and food for the sloth.** • It takes 30 days for a sloth to digest a single leaf. • **Female sloths can give birth to a single baby a year, and they take care of their young for at least six months.** • Sloths are mostly solitary, meaning they live alone. • **For the most part, sloths are nocturnal, meaning they are mainly active at night.** • A sloth can hold its breath for 40 minutes underwater. • **A number of different insects, including moths, cockroaches, and beetles, live on a sloth's fur.** • Prehistoric sloths were 12-foot (3.6 m)-tall giants with razor-sharp claws. They lived on the ground, not in trees. • **There are two main types of sloths: two-toed sloths and three-toed sloths.** • Two-toed sloths eat plants but sometimes consume insects and bird eggs. Three-toed sloths are herbivores; they only eat plants. • **A sloth's fur grows from its belly toward its back. Because sloths are almost always upside down, this helps water roll off their bodies when it rains.** • Sloths live in the rain forests of Central and South America. • **Three-toed sloths have markings on their faces that make them look like they're always smiling.** • Sloths give birth in the trees. • **The species of algae that grows on sloths is called** *Trichophilus welckeri.* **It can only be found**

A two-toed sloth eating flowers. Flowers are part of a sloth's diet.

on the fur of sloths. • Sloths can turn their heads 270 degrees. • **A sloth's organs are attached to its rib cage so they don't get squished while the animal is upside down.** • Two-toed sloths actually have three toes on each foot but two fingers on each hand. • **Sloths have existed on Earth for about 64 million years.** • Baby sloths cling to their mothers after they're born. After a few months, the young sloths start hanging upside down from the trees. • **Sloths have curved claws.** • It would take more than a month for a sloth to walk 1 mile (1.6 km). • **If threatened by a predator, a sloths will scratch and bite.** • A sloth's teeth grow throughout its whole life. • **The average claw of a sloth is 3 to 4 inches (7.5–10 cm) long.** • Birds known as brown jays eat insects off the fur of three-toed sloths. • **A sloth's large stomach has four chambers.** • Some sloths have been known to stay hanging upside down even after death. • **A sloth can poop a third of its body weight in a single trip to the bathroom.** • All sloths are color-blind. • **Scientists think sloths might be able to turn off their metabolism—the body's chemical reactions that turn food into energy—when the temperature is too hot or too cold.** • Sloths have a very good sense of smell. • **If a sloth gets too cold, its stomach won't be able to digest food, causing the sloth to starve.** • Sloths can fall 100 feet (30 m) to the ground without getting hurt.

An illustration of a giant ground sloth during the Ice Age

SLOTHS SWIM THREE TIMES FASTER THAN THEY CRAWL.

Cool Cetaceans

A narwhal's tusk is covered with holes and contains lots of nerves.

65 Totally Random Facts About WHALES

Whales are mammals, so unlike fish, they can't breathe underwater. • There are two types of whales: baleen and toothed. • **Toothed whales are hunters, preying on fish, squid, and sea creatures.** • Dolphins are a type of toothed whale. • **There are 76 species of toothed whales and 14 baleen whale species.** • Baleen whales are bigger than toothed whales—except for the sperm whale, which is the largest toothed whale. • **Baleen whales have two holes on the top of their heads and toothed whales have one.** • Whales use their blowholes like nostrils to help them breathe. • **At up to 330,000 pounds (150,000 kg), a blue whale weighs about as much as 24 elephants.** • A narwhal's

MALE HUMPBACK WHALES SING COMPLEX SONGS THAT CAN LAST UP TO 20 MINUTES.

Humpback whale breaching

Amazon pink river dolphins have molar-like teeth in the back of their mouths used to crunch food. Other dolphins don't have such teeth.

tusk can grow to be 10 feet (3 m) long. • **Porpoises have spade-shaped teeth.** • Dolphins evolved from land animals that once had legs. That's why they move their tails up and down when they swim, instead of side to side. • **Nicknamed "sea canaries," belugas are noisy whales that communicate with whistles, clicks, and chirps.** • Gray whales migrate about 10,000 miles (16,000 km) round-trip, one of the longest migrations of any mammal. • **The smallest baleen whale in North American waters is the 20,000-pound (9,000-kg) minke whale.** • A sperm whale's head makes up 40 percent of its body length. These whales have the biggest brains of any animal on Earth. • **Bottlenose dolphins sleep with half of their brain at a time and keep one eye open to watch for predators.** • The deepest-diving animal is the Cuvier's beaked whale. It can dive 1.9 miles (3 km) deep and stay submerged for more than two hours. • **Whales are related to hippos.** • Dolphins don't chew their food; they swallow it whole. • **Whales migrate to follow their food, give birth, and even shed their skin.** • Toothed whales can teach and learn from one another. • **The pygmy sperm whale is about the size of a dolphin.** • To escape predators, the pygmy sperm whale blasts a brown liquid out of its body to create a cloud so it can disappear. • **Belugas and narwhals are born gray and lighten as they grow older.** • Narwhals have a unicorn-like tusk that's actually a very long tooth. • **Blue whales have a comblike mouth with 300 to 400 bony plates to sift food from the water.** • At birth, a blue whale is about 26 feet (8 m) long and weighs up to 6,000 pounds (2,720 kg). • **Humpback whales are about the size of a school bus.** • Dolphins have cone-shaped teeth. •

Beluga whale

UNLIKE OTHER WHALES, BELUGAS HAVE FLEXIBLE NECKS THAT ALLOW THEM TO TURN THEIR HEADS.

Female dolphins are pregnant for between 9 and 16 months and have one baby at a time. ● Bowhead whales, which live in the Arctic, can live for more than 200 years. ● **Fin whales, the second largest mammals on Earth, sometimes mate with blue whales.** ● Some dolphins have only 14 teeth, while others can have 240. ● **Baleen whales usually live alone, but they stay connected by listening to each other underwater.** ● The largest dolphin is the orca, or killer whale. Males grow up to 32 feet (9.8 m) and weigh up to 22,000 pounds (9,000 kg). ● **Baby orcas are 7 to 8 feet (2.1 to 2.4 m) long.** ● At about 4 to 5 feet (1.2 to 1.5 m) long, the Hector's dolphin is the smallest dolphin in the world. ● **Harbor porpoises make a sneeze-like puffing sound when they breathe.** ● Dolphins can live between 20 and 80 years. ● **Orcas are the only dolphins to live in Arctic and Antarctic waters.** ● Common minke whales each have a unique color that scientists can use to identify different individuals. ● **A group of**

A whale's tail fins are called its flukes.

dolphins is called a pod. ● Pods travel in groups of up to 30 members. ● **Right whales and bowheads are skimmers, and they gather food by swimming slowly, open mouthed through dense patches of tiny animals.** ● Most dolphins live in the ocean, but four species of river dolphins live only in the Amazon River and a few species live in rivers in Asia. ● **Bottlenose dolphins swallow fish headfirst so the food doesn't get stuck in their throats.** ● When hunting, dolphins blow bubbles to herd their prey to the surface. ● **Orcas stay with their mothers for life.** ● Dolphins use a hunting technique called "fish-whacking." They hit fish with their tails to stun them so they're easier to catch. ● **Like elephants, bottlenose dolphins can recognize themselves in a mirror.** ● Sometimes dolphins fit sponges over their beaks to protect themselves from sharp rocks as they hunt for fish. ● **Dolphins sometimes swim alongside ships and ride the waves to save energy.**

The World's Largest Animal!

AT NEARLY 100 FEET (30 M) LONG, THE BLUE WHALE IS THE LARGEST ANIMAL EVER TO HAVE LIVED ON EARTH. Its heart alone can weigh 400 pounds (181 kg), and a blue whale's tongue is so long that 11 people could stand across it. **Despite their massive size, blue whales feed on tiny marine life—shrimplike animals called krill.** Not surprisingly, whales need a lot of krill to sustain their size. **A single adult can consume 6,000 to 8,000 pounds (2,720–3,630 kg) of krill a day.** Scientists believe these gigantic creatures live for about 90 years.

DOLPHINS COMMUNICATE WITH CLICKS, WHISTLES, SQUAWKS, MOANS, GROANS, YELPS, BARKS, AND SQUEALS.

A pod of spinner dolphins swims in the Red Sea.

A humpback whale feeds at the surface of the water.

Scientists call this bow-riding. • During their four-month migration, blue whales barely eat, surviving on their reserves of blubber. • **Mother dolphins teach their offspring how to hunt.** • Male humpback dolphins in Australia offer sponges to attract mates. • **Unlike other porpoise species, the Yangtze finless porpoise lives in fresh water— China's Yangtze River.** • A blue whale calf can drink more than 50 gallons (189 L) of its mother's milk every day. • **Whale poop is food for tiny marine algae called phytoplankton, which make about half the world's oxygen.** • Dolphins track prey using echolocation. They bounce sound off their prey to identify its position.

Slink, Slither,

FROGS WERE THE FIRST
LAND ANIMALS TO HAVE
VOCAL CORDS.

Red-eyed
tree frog

and Hop

Gila monster

More than 11,000 species of reptiles are found around the world.

There are four main groups of reptiles: Crocodilia (crocodiles and alligators), Squamata (lizards and snakes), Testudines (turtles), and Sphenodontia (tuataras).

Amphibians lived on Earth 128 million years before dinosaurs.

The majority of reptiles are snakes and lizards.

Most female frogs are bigger than males.

Reptiles have been on Earth for more than 315 million years.

Amphibians include frogs, salamanders, and caecilians.

One of the largest land animals (and reptiles) to ever roam the planet was the 115-foot (35 m)-long dinosaur *Argentinosaurus*.

Reptiles were the dominant animals during the Mesozoic era, which lasted for 185 million years until the dinosaurs went extinct.

The world's largest bullfrog is the goliath bullfrog, weighing in at 7 pounds (3 kg). When vocalizing, this frog makes a whistling noise.

An amphibian lives in water as a baby but develops lungs and breathes air as an adult.

The word *amphibian* means "two lives," referring to how the creature develops and lives: first life in water, then on land.

Native to the southern United States, the American alligator is one of the largest living reptiles in the world.

Mexican dumpy frogs live in tree canopies and don't spend much time on the ground.

With the exception of crocs, most reptiles must hold their breath while swallowing.

The green anaconda is the largest snake on Earth.

Gila monsters are poisonous.

All reptiles are covered in dry, scaly skin and regularly shed their skin.

Desert tortoises dig grooves into the ground to collect rainwater to drink.

The younger the reptile, the more often it sheds its skin.

Toads are a type of frog with warty, dry skin and shorter hind legs.

Snakes shed their skin in one whole section, like a shirt sleeve.

Two weeks before shedding its skin, a snake will stop eating.

About once a week, a frog will shed its skin and eat it.

SNAKES DESCENDED FROM RELATIVES THAT ONCE HAD FOUR LIMBS.

Pit viper

Unlike mammals and birds, reptiles cannot maintain their own body temperature. They bask in the sun to warm up.

Some nonpoisonous frogs developed colorful skin to make them look like they might be poisonous to trick predators into leaving them alone.

The temperature of the environment directly affects how a reptile digests its food and reproduces.

Most reptiles lay eggs in a nest and leave the young to fend for themselves.

Reptiles become inactive during colder months to conserve energy.

The temperature of the soil determines whether eggs of crocodiles and most turtles will be born male or female.

The desert tortoise lays eggs the size of Ping-Pong balls. Babies are only 2 inches (5 cm) long when they hatch.

Boa constrictors and most vipers and pit vipers give birth to live young.

Ornate horned frogs are not good at chasing food, so they bury themselves and eat what walks by.

Within hours after birth, baby reptiles are ready to hunt.

Compared with mammals' brains, reptiles' brains are much smaller relative to their body size.

Despite their smaller brains, reptiles in captivity have learned to solve problems, opening doors with hinges and prying off jar lids.

The bumps on an alligator's body makes it look like a log floating in the water.

Frogs have lived on Earth for 200 million years.

Reptiles defend themselves from predators using camouflage, hissing, and biting. Some also have a poison or venom that they use to attack enemies or prey.

Red toad

Each time a **RATTLESNAKE** sheds its skin, a new segment gets added to its rattle.

Tuatara

Alligators have rounded snouts. When they close the top of thier mouths, their teeth show.

Tuataras, found in New Zealand, can breathe as little as one breath per hour while resting.

Frogs use their eyes to help push down their food when they eat.

A herpetologist is a scientist who studies reptiles and amphibians.

Some desert-dwelling reptiles can store water in their bladders for several months.

Many reptiles, like snakes, do not chew their food. They swallow it whole.

Because they are cold-blooded, reptiles are more often found in warmer climates where there is more sunlight.

Reptiles come in a broad range of sizes, from less than 1 inch (25 mm) to nearly 20 feet (6 m).

Frogs can jump more than 20 times their body length.

The largest reptile on record is the saltwater crocodile, which can reach about 20 feet (6 m) long and weigh up to 2,900 pounds (1,315 kg).

The goliath bullfrog can leap 10 feet (3 m) in a single bound.

The ancestors of crocodiles roamed Earth more than 200 million years ago.

The crocodile is the fiercest freshwater predator. It crushes its prey and swallows it whole.

Crocodiles can survive a year without eating.

A croc's stomach is so powerful it can digest bones, hooves, and shells.

Even though crocs mostly live alone, they form long-term relationships with each other to raise young and hunt.

GIANT TORTOISES can live between 150 and 250 years!

Like birds, some reptiles swallow rocks to help digest their food.

The Komodo dragon can play.

Snakes can see infrared light; mammals, including humans, can't.

African bullfrogs can stay buried for years waiting for rain.

Reptiles tend to live longer than mammals.

Caimans can live up to 60 years.

Alligator snapping turtles can live up to 70 years.

Some frog croaks are so loud that they can be heard up to 1 mile (1.6 km) away.

American alligators can live up to 80 years in captivity.

Some frogs can eat a mouse in one gulp.

Nile crocodiles can live up to 100 years.

Fire salamander

POISONOUS FROGS ARE BRIGHTLY COLORED TO WARN PREDATORS TO STAY AWAY.

Tuataras have the slowest growth rate of any reptiles and keep growing until they are 35 years old.

Male American gators can weigh about 1,000 pounds (454 kg) and can reach up to 15 feet (4.5 m) in length.

Salamanders are silent.

Salamanders are deaf.

Nearly a fifth of all reptiles are considered endangered.

The reticulated python is the longest reptile in the world, stretching 32 feet (10 m) in length.

Shingleback skinks mate for life.

It's a myth that you can get a wart from an amphibian.

The horned toad is actually a lizard, not a toad or frog.

Unlike turtles, tortoises live only on land.

The Colombian four-eyed frog only has two eyes (the other two are actually just large spots to trick predators).

When grabbed by a predator, the smoky jungle frog screams until it is released.

Tuataras are the last surviving members of a group of reptiles that lived more than 200 million years ago.

Wallace's flying frogs, which live in Malaysia and Borneo, can glide through the air for 50 feet (15 m) or more.

Tadpoles are also called polliwogs.

Snakes have up to 585 vertebrae in their backs; humans have 33.

Frogs have excellent night vision.

Python snakes shiver on top of their eggs to warm them.

Constrictor snakes kill their prey by cutting off their blood supply.

This Turtle Stinks!

THE STINKPOT TURTLE HAS DIFFERENT NAMES, including the common musk turtle and the eastern musk turtle. But no matter what you call it, this turtle stinks! This small species, which can fit in the palm of your hand, lives in the eastern United States and southeastern Canada. It also has an unusual ability: **blasting a strong, musky scent from the base of its tail.** It spends most of its time in muddy streams, creeks, and ponds, and walks around **looking for crayfish, clams, snails, fish, tadpoles, and insects to eat.** However, if a predator such as a skunk, bird, fox, or even a fish wants to make a meal out of it, it has a unique defense: When the turtle is startled, **glands near its tail will shoot out an orange-colored liquid** that smells like very strong armpit odor!

Milk snake hatching

Flying lizards have skin flaps between their ribs that they use as wings.

There are more than 7,000 species of frogs.

The female Suriname toad of South America carries her young inside her skin on her back.

Unlike most toads that have bumpy skin, the smooth-sided toad does not.

Female American bullfrogs lay 20,000 eggs at a time.

Amphibians have no hair or scales, and most lay their eggs in water.

There are 215 species of caecilians, legless amphibians that live underground or in water.

Though most frogs live in fresh water, a few species can survive in salt water.

The 5-foot (1.5 m) Chinese giant salamander is the largest of all amphibians.

The wood frog, which lives in the Arctic Circle, can survive with 65 percent of its body frozen.

Borneo eared frogs create foam nests that hang over the water for their eggs.

There are more than 700 species of salamanders.

The tuatara can live for more than 100 years.

Australian tree frogs can make smells like roasted cashews and rotting meat to repel insects.

Crocodiles can't move their tongues.

Geckos use their tongues to lick their eyeballs clean.

Frogs are the only amphibians without tails and necks.

Tadpoles are born with gills, just like a fish.

Sea snakes are poisonous.

To attract a mate, male smoky jungle frogs stand at the edge of the water and call out.

Crocodiles can't chew.

Some reptiles that live in desert climates have an extra-large bladder. It allows the reptile to store water for a few months.

The gastric brooding frog swallows her fertilized eggs, which grow in her stomach for eight weeks and then hop out of her mouth.

MANY GECKOS CHIRP, CLICK, AND BARK EITHER TO ATTRACT A MATE OR TO DEFEND THEIR TERRITORY.

Turn to page 223 for the answers!

559 Totally Random Facts About

Planet Earth

Hurricanes, Waterfalls, Earthquakes, and Eruptions

Africa is the only continent that is in all four hemispheres: Northern, Southern, Western, and Eastern. • **Istanbul, a city in Turkey, sits on two continents: Asia and Europe.** • Mauna Kea is roughly 33,500 feet (10,211 m) tall from its base, which starts below sea level, to its top, more than 3,000 feet (914 m) taller than Mount Everest. From sea level, Mount Everest is the highest mountain in the world. • **The United States and Canada share the longest border in the world.** • A harbor in Copenhagen, Denmark, has a statue of the Little Mermaid. • **The Sahara desert, stretching across 11 countries, is about as large as the United States.** • The Andes in South America are the world's longest mountain range on land, stretching 5,500 miles (8,850 km) from north to south. • **The largest active volcano in the world is Hawaii's Mauna Loa.** • The Nile is the longest river in the world, running about 4,130 miles (6,650 km) from end to end. • **The four largest countries by size are Russia, Canada, China, and the United States.** •

Globe-trotting

99 Totally Random Facts About GEOGRAPHY

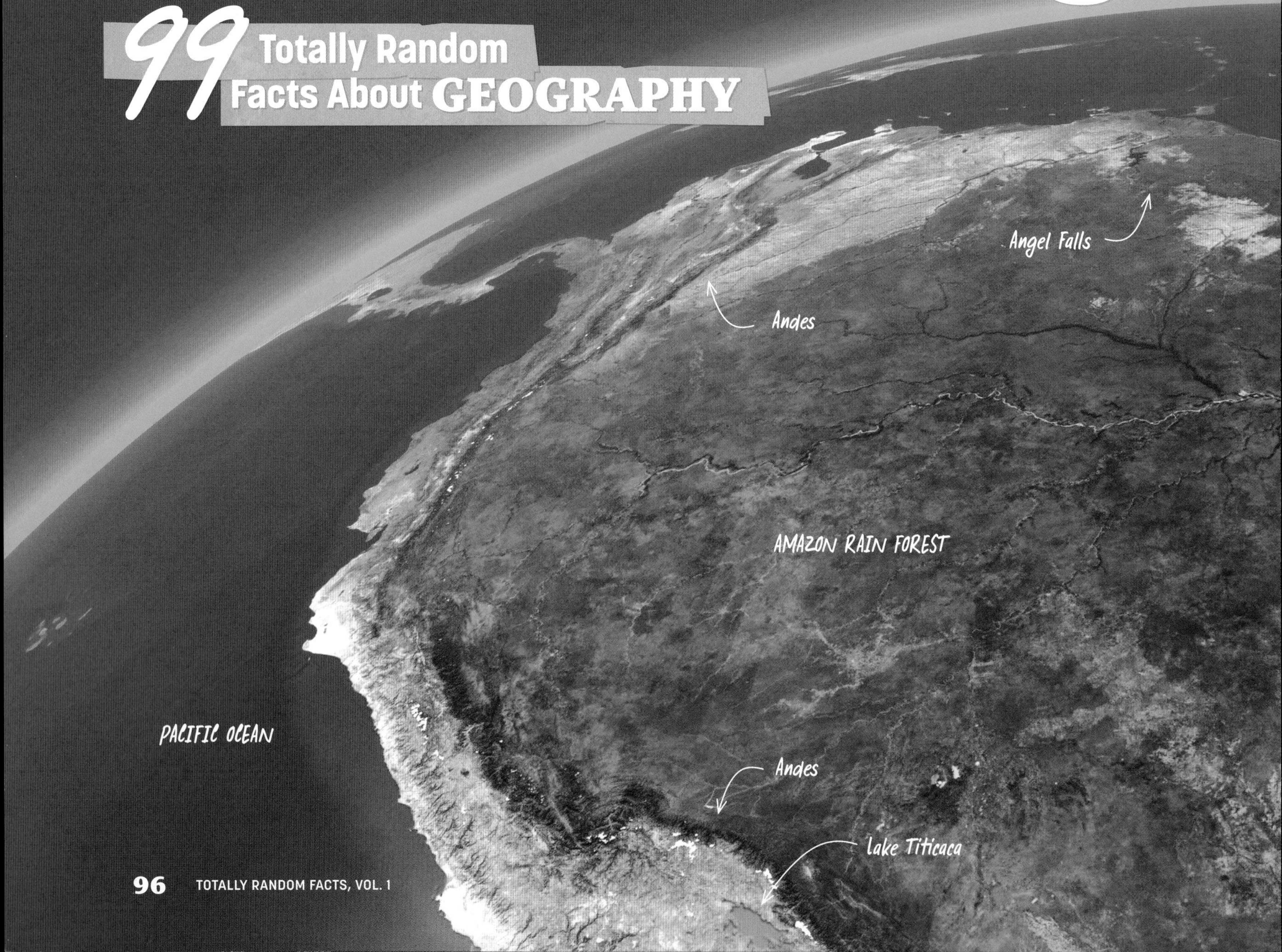

Angel Falls

Andes

AMAZON RAIN FOREST

PACIFIC OCEAN

Andes

Lake Titicaca

The flag of Nepal

Asia is the planet's most populated continent, with 60 percent of the world's population calling it home. • **Germany is the most populated country in Europe, with a population of 82 million.** • Nepal is the only country that has a flag that's not quadrilateral, or four-sided. • **There are seven continents and five oceans on our planet.** • Africa has 54 countries, making it the continent with the most countries. • **Africa is known as "the cradle of humankind" because it's where the oldest human bones have been discovered.** • The highest waterfall in the world is Angel Falls in Venezuela. • **The largest island in the world is Greenland, which belongs to the country of Denmark.** • In Palau's Jellyfish Lake, millions of golden jellyfish swim across the water each day. • **The two smallest countries in the world, Vatican City and Monaco, are both in Europe.** • The full name of the United Kingdom is United Kingdom of Great Britain and Northern Ireland. • **More people live in the U.S. state of California than in the entire country of Canada.** • Australia is the only country that is also a continent. • **Antarctica is the continent with the smallest population. Mainly scientists live there and only for short periods of time.** • Up to 90 percent of Earth's ice is in Antarctica. • **The Sahara is the world's largest nonpolar desert.** • Mozambique is the only country name with all five vowels. • **Vulcan Point in the Philippines is an island within a lake, on an island within a lake, on an island.** • As Earth's tectonic plates move, the Pacific Ocean gets smaller. • **Both Russia and China border 14 countries.** • The Sargasso Sea is the only sea with no coasts. It's surrounded by ocean currents. • **There is an active supervolcano under Yellowstone National Park.**

Kerepakupai Merú (Angel Falls), Venezuela

AMAZON RAIN FOREST

ATLANTIC OCEAN

The Amazon rain forest produces more than **20 PERCENT OF THE WORLD'S OXYGEN.**

With more than 200 known pyramids, Sudan has more pyramids than Egypt. • **Middle Island, the southernmost point of Ontario, Canada, is at the same latitude as Northern California.** • The U.S. state of Kentucky has the longest cave system in the world. • **The deepest place on Earth is called Challenger Deep. It's located in the Mariana Trench of the Pacific Ocean, 35,814 feet (10,916 m) below the surface.** • Crater Lake in Oregon, U.S.A., formed after a 12,000-foot (3,658-m) volcano collapsed close to 8,000 years ago.

 The longest place-name in the United States is **LAKE CHARGOGGAGOGGMANCHAUGGAGOGGCHAUBUNAGUNGAMAUGG** in Massachusetts.

• **With nearly 32,000 lakes, Canada has more lakes than any other country in the world.** • At 11,913 feet (3,631 m) above sea level, La Paz, Bolivia, is the highest capital city in the world. • **The Empire State Building in New York City gets so much mail that it has its own zip code.** • The North Pole is an island made of ice caps. • **Iceland grows by 2 inches (5 cm) every year.** • About 90 percent of the world's population lives in the Northern Hemisphere. • **Point Nemo is the most remote place on Earth. It's 1,000 miles (1,600 km) from land in any direction.** • More than half of the world's freshwater supply is from Antarctica. • **It takes** about three months for water from Lake Itasca, Minnesota, U.S.A., the source of the Mississippi River, to flow downriver to the Gulf of Mexico. • The surface level of the Dead Sea drops by about 3 feet (91 cm) every year. • **Your feet will bob to the water's surface in the Dead Sea. That's because it's eight to nine times saltier than the typical ocean.** • In winter, you could walk from Alaska, in the United States, to Russia when a 2.5-mile (4 km)-wide stretch of

The country with the most coastline is **CANADA,** totaling 125,567 miles (202,080 km) long.

Canada's Bay of Fundy has the highest tidal range in the world.

water freezes. ● **The world's largest collection of maps— over 5 million—is housed in the U.S. Library of Congress in Washington, D.C.** ● Middle Eastern countries import sand from Australia, which works better for construction. ● **Nearly 850 languages are spoken in Papua New Guinea.** ● The Great Barrier Reef has a heart-shaped reef. ● **On Lake Titicaca in Peru, some people live on floating islands.** ● In Tanzania, salt-loving microorganisms turn Lake Natron's salty surface a deep shade of red. ● **A town in Nebraska, U.S.A., only has one resident.**

Heart Reef in the Great Barrier Reef

The World's Tallest Mountain Is Still Growing!

MOUNT EVEREST, IN THE HIMALAYA RANGE TOWERING ABOVE NEPAL AND CHINA, holds the record for the highest mountain peak at 29,029 feet (8,848 m). And guess what? It's still growing at 16 inches (41 cm) per century. Roughly 50 million years ago, the mountain formed when the Indian and Eurasian tectonic plates collided. Even today, **this upward force is pushing Everest's summit about a quarter of an inch (63 mm) higher each year.** If you're wondering what's on top of the mountain, don't be expecting a lot of wildlife. One of the highest living animal species is the jumping spider, which can be found at 22,000 feet (6,700 m), and certain birds like bar-headed geese have been seen flying over the summit. If you're curious about the view, you'll need a lot of preparation and resources. First of all, **it takes an average of 12 weeks to adapt yourself to the high altitude,** where breathing will be difficult because the air is so thin. This requires training by moving between the base camps over and over again. Then you'll have to get ready for the harsh climate. **The warmest temperature there is –4°F (–20°C).** From 17,400 feet (5,300 m) and up, the mountain is capped year-round with snow and ice. Finally, you'll have to save up. You'll spend at least $30,000 on transportation, guides, training, and professional gear to climb the mountain.

The world's northernmost capital city is Reykjavik, Iceland. **Saudi Arabia is 95 percent desert.** Ecuador and Chile are the only countries in South America that don't border Brazil. **On average, men from Amsterdam are taller than men in any other country.** Alaska has some of the largest cities by area in the United States. Sitka, for example, is 2,800 square miles (7,252 sq km). **It would take seven days on a train to cross the length of Russia.** Snow fell in the Sahara desert in 1979, 2016, and 2018. **Iceland has both icequakes and earthquakes.** Antarctica's Dry Valleys haven't had any rain or snow in nearly 2 million years. **In 2008, mountain climbers took the Olympic torch to the top of Mount Everest.** Palm Jumeirah in Dubai is a giant human-made archipelago shaped like a palm tree. **Australia is home to 21 of the world's 25 most venomous snakes.** The top of Mount Everest has cell phone reception. **There's a village in France called Y.** The world's largest outdoor snowball fight, with more than 7,600 participants, occurred in Canada in 2016. **Including France's overseas territories,**

Sulfur lake in Dallol, Ethiopia

France occupies 12 time zones. Hundreds of years ago, a lake called Mega Chad in the Sahara desert was the size of England. **Small icebergs are sometimes called bergy bits or growlers.** Indonesia has more coral reefs than any other country. **Dallol, Ethiopia, is the hottest inhabited place on Earth. Average temperatures reach 106°F (41°C).** The Grand Canyon covers an area of about 1,900 square

Australian common death adder

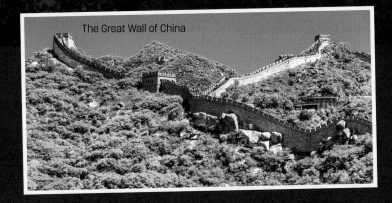
The Great Wall of China

miles (4921 sq km), making it larger than the state of Rhode Island. ● **Antarctica is almost entirely covered in desert.** ● Asia's Lake Baikal has 1,500 plant and animal species found nowhere else on Earth. ● **In the past 100 years, Mexico City has sunk 26 feet (8 m).** ● In Alaska, U.S.A., there are 100-foot (30 m)-tall sand dunes. ● **The Philippines is made up of some 7,100 islands.** ● The deepest dug hole in the world is the Kola well in Russia, reaching more than 40,000 feet (12,192 m) underground. ● **The Great Wall of China, the world's longest human-made structure, took more than 1,800 years to build. Sticky rice was used to help hold it together.** ● Russia crosses 11 different time zones. ● **During summer, water** gushing from Niagara Falls could fill 13,000 bathtubs per second. ● The longest war memorial is the 151-mile (243 km) Great Ocean Road in Australia. It was dedicated to the fallen Allied soldiers of World War II. ● **Portugal has land in North America, Africa, and Europe.** ● The Barberton Greenstone Belt in South Africa is 3.6 billion years old, making it the world's oldest mountain range. ● **Slovenia's Lake Cerknica disappears every year. It's filled each autumn with fresh rainfall, which drains through underground sinkholes.** ● The Trans-Siberian Railway in Russia crosses 3,901 bridges. ● **Ireland didn't use postal codes until 2015.** ● The world's longest bridge, located in China, is 102 miles (164 km) long. ● **The Great Blue Hole off the coast of Belize is the world's largest sinkhole. It measures 984 feet (300 m) wide and is more than 400 feet (122 m) deep.** ● Your nails grow at roughly the same rate that our continents move.

The largest capital city in the world is **TOKYO, JAPAN,** with a population of 38 million people.

Get Wind of

Fire tornado

Every snowflake has six sides.

Moonbows are rainbows that form from moonlight.

Thor, the god of thunder in Norse mythology, was believed to make thunder by banging on clouds with his hammer.

A heat wave lasts for at least five straight days.

Meteorologists are scientists who study the weather and the atmosphere.

Tornadoes made of fire, called fire devils, can reach 2000°F (1093°C).

Volcanic eruptions can cause lightning.

Commonwealth Bay, Antarctica, is the windiest place on the planet.

A 2-mile (3.2-km)-high dust storm once traveled 2,000 miles (3,220 km) to the East Coast, swallowing monuments like the Empire State Building and the White House.

The average thunderstorm releases more energy than an atomic bomb.

Every minute, 2,000 thunderstorms splatter down on our planet.

Blood-red algae once fell like rain in Kerala, India.

A single snowflake needs about 100,000 tiny cloud droplets to form.

Heat waves can cause highways to buckle and train tracks to bend.

About 900 Burmese pythons once escaped into the Florida Everglades during a hurricane.

The most accurate temperatures are read using a thermometer away from direct sunlight, at exactly 4.9 feet (1.5 m) above the ground.

When a flood is coming, worms crawl to the surface to breathe.

This

144 Totally Random Facts About **WEATHER**

TORNADO ALLEY, IN THE CENTRAL UNITED STATES, SEES MORE SWIRLING CYCLONES THAN ANY OTHER PLACE ON EARTH.

White-lipped tree frog

Hurricane winds can push waves as tall as giraffes onto shore.

Snow can fall so thickly in Antarctica that, if someone stood right in front you, you wouldn't be able to see them.

Rescuers made mittens for koalas injured by wildfires in Australia.

Water boils at 212°F (100°C) at sea level.

The hottest temperature ever recorded on Earth was 134.1°F (56.7°C). It was in Furnace Creek, California, U.S.A., in 1913.

The coldest temperature ever recorded on Earth was –128.6°F (–89.2°C) at Vostok Station in Antarctica in 1983.

By counting a cricket's chirps, you can estimate the temperature: The colder it is, the fewer times per minute they chirp.

Warmer autumns often mean fatter spiders.

A landslide in Norway once swept eight buildings into the sea.

In Iran, 200 villages were once completely buried by 26 feet (8 m)

Some toads and frogs croak louder just before it rains.

The common raindrop is shaped like a hamburger bun.

A cloud is a mass of tiny water droplets, ice crystals, and other particles suspended in the air.

Fish, birds, snakes, and frogs have all rained from the sky after being sucked up by rotating columns of water called waterspouts.

There are three temperature scales: Fahrenheit, Celsius, and Kelvin.

Cats and dogs can sense when a storm is coming.

Only five countries use Fahrenheit as their official temperature scale.

Pinecones can predict the weather. In wet weather they close, and in dry weather they open.

The world's highest weather station is on top of Mount Everest, 27,657 feet (8,430 m) above sea level.

Differences in atmospheric pressure, the pressure caused by the weight of the atmosphere, creates wind.

A hurricane seen from space

Thin, wispy cirrus clouds are formed by ice crystals.

Air feels warmer in the sun than in the shade.

Water freezes at 32°F (0°C).

Sleet bounces off the ground, while freezing rain sticks to it.

About 90 percent of wildfires are caused by humans.

In 1953, meteorologists in the United States started naming hurricanes and tropical storms.

Hurricane names alternate between male and female.

A fulminologist is someone who studies lightning.

Fog, mist, and dew can all create rainbows.

The average global temperature has risen 1.7°F (0.94°C) since 1880.

Zeus was the sky and thunder god in Greek mythology.

There are nine common types of rainbows.

Tornadoes, cyclones, twisters, and whirlwinds are all different names for columns of rapidly rotating air.

Each year, a person has a one in 500,000 chance of being struck by lightning.

In a primary rainbow, the most common kind, the sky under the arch is brighter than the sky above it.

THE SHAPE OF A RAINBOW IS A FULL CIRCLE, BUT FROM THE GROUND WE ONLY SEE THE PART ABOVE THE HORIZON.

Wind is silent until it brushes against something.

You always see lightning before you hear thunder. That's because light travels much faster than sound.

A billion tons of rain fall on Earth every minute.

A blizzard is a snowstorm with fast winds and low visibility.

Fossils with imprints of raindrops from 2.7 billion years ago were discovered in India.

The World Weather Watch uses ocean buoys to collect data.

Hurricanes gather strength from warm water. That's why they often start in tropical areas.

The human eye sees seven colors in a rainbow, always in the same order.

When warm air rises from Earth, the water vapor in the air cools into droplets and ice crystals, forming a cloud.

A typical lightning flash is 1 inch (2.5 cm) wide.

A boom of thunder is about as loud as a jet plane taking off.

A single cloud can contain a million gallons (3.8 million L) of water.

Hail only develops in thunderstorms.

In 350 B.C., the Greek philosopher Aristotle became one of the first people to study rainbows.

Hailstones

The hazy halo you see around the sun is formed by high cirrostratus clouds.

During a flood, a car can float in as little as 1 foot (30 cm) of water.

Raindrops plop down to Earth at speeds between 12 and 20 miles an hour (24 and 32 kmh).

Big, puffy cumulus clouds exist for only 5 to 40 minutes.

Some blizzards can have wind speeds as strong as a hurricane.

A molecule of water will hang in the air for about 10 to 12 days.

The visible arch of a rainbow is always formed at the same angle.

An average of 2,000 active thunderstorms are happening right now around the world.

Fog can produce snow.

People skied in the streets during Snowmageddon, a major blizzard that blew through the northeastern United States in 2010.

The air surrounding a lightning bolt is five times hotter than the surface of the sun.

A snowflake up close

A tornado's funnel can be a mile (1.6 km) wide.

Before the 19th century, people believed that thunder was caused by clouds crashing together.

Snowflakes can take up to an hour to reach the ground.

Dirty snow melts faster than clean snow.

The driest continent on Earth is Antarctica. It receives the least rain or snow.

Nephology is the study of clouds.

When hurricanes make landfall, they rapidly lose strength because of the lack of moisture.

The sound of thunder comes from a sonic shock wave produced by lightning.

Rainbows happen when sunlight passes through rain droplets.

The most common form of lightning never leaves the cloud.

Cumulonimbus clouds cause tornadoes, lightning, and hail.

A rainbow is not a physical object. It's an optical phenomenon.

The word *blizzard* was first used in the 1870s by an Iowa newspaper.

When two rainbows occur together, it's called a double rainbow. This happens when light is reflected twice inside the same water droplets.

It's possible to see a lightning bolt without ever hearing thunder.

The Great Plains and upper Midwest of the United States have more blizzards than the rest of the country.

When it's summer in Australia, it's winter in the United States.

A rain forest receives between 98 and 177 inches (250 and 450 cm) of rain each year.

Lightning Is Shocking!

LIGHTNING IS A POWERFUL FORM OF ELECTRICITY. Have you ever gotten a shock touching a metal door handle after rubbing your feet on carpet? That's static electricity. Lightning is much, much hotter. The temperature of lightning is about 54,000°F (30,000°C). **That's about five times hotter than the surface of the sun!** Surprisingly, all that heat starts with ice crystals. Lightning originates in cumulonimbus, or thunderhead, clouds filled with water droplets and ice crystals. The droplets and crystals bump around in the cloud, creating positive and negative electrical charges. The positive charges rise to the top of the cloud, while the negative charges sink to the bottom. The negative charges build up and start generating positive charges on whatever is standing down on Earth, like a tall tree or building. Because opposites attract, **the negative charge in the cloud and the positive charge on Earth start to connect and create a circuit.** Eventually the charge gets so strong that—WHAM!—it causes a bolt of electricity that zooms out at 62 miles an hour (100 kmh).

"Crown fires" happen when wind carries a wildfire quickly through treetops.

Hurricanes have three main sections: the eye, the eye wall, and rain bands.

Two feet (60 cm) of rushing floodwater can carry away a pickup truck.

South America, Africa, and Asia are home to most of Earth's rain forests.

In 2006, a man in Missouri, U.S.A., survived being carried 1,307 feet (398 m) by a tornado.

A thunderstorm usually lifts more than 200 million gallons (757 million L) of water into Earth's atmosphere. That's enough to fill 300 Olympic-size swimming pools.

A mirage is an optical illusion. What looks like water is actually a reflection of the sky shimmering on a layer of hot air above the ground.

In 1752, Benjamin Franklin flew a kite during a thunderstorm to prove electricity was a natural phenomenon.

EACH SECOND, THERE ARE ABOUT 50 LIGHTNING STRIKES AROUND THE WORLD.

"Roy G. Biv" is an acronym for the colors of the rainbow: red, orange, yellow, green, blue, indigo, and violet.

Brontophobia is the fear of thunder. Many dogs suffer from it.

Tornadoes form in the base of a cloud before touching down on land.

Lightning zooms 540 times faster than an airplane.

The award for the greatest one-minute rainfall goes to Unionville, Maryland, U.S.A., for dumping 1.23 inches (31.2 mm) of rain.

Thick, gray nimbostratus clouds block the sun and make rain.

Lightning strikes can cause wildfires.

The fear of thunder and lightning is called astraphobia.

There are thunderstorms in space. Scientists have observed them on the planets Jupiter, Neptune, Saturn, Uranus, and Venus.

Newfoundland, Canada, has over 200 foggy days every year. It's the foggiest place on Earth.

Thundersnow happens when thunder and lightning are produced during a winter snowstorm.

Hailstones can fall at speeds of up to 40 miles an hour (64 km).

The world's tallest snowman, towering at 125 feet (38 m), was built in Austria in 2020. Its nickname was Riesi, which means "giant" in English.

There are at least 10 different cloud types.

Fake fog machines are commonly used for Broadway plays and Halloween parties.

During the American War for Independence, a heavy cloak of fog helped George Washington retreat to safety from the British during the Battle of Long Island in 1776.

The word *hurricane* comes from the Maya god Huracan who created storm, fire, and wind.

When a tornado forms above Earth's surface without touching down, it creates a funnel cloud.

Rainbows at night are called lunar rainbows. They are very rare.

FOG IS BASICALLY A CLOUD CLOSE TO THE GROUND.

North of the equator, hurricanes spin counterclockwise. South of the equator, they spin clockwise.

Flooding causes up to 90 percent of all natural disasters in the United States.

Large hail sometimes falls before a tornado.

Because of an ice jam, Niagara Falls, on the U.S.-Canada border, stopped gushing for nearly two days in 1948.

From up close, a lightning bolt sounds like a cracking whip. From farther away, it sounds like a low rumble.

By counting the seconds between lightning and thunder, you can calculate your distance from the lightning bolt. Every five seconds equals 1 mile (1.6 km).

Fogbow

Fogbows—rainbows made with fog—are usually white, red, and blue.

There are at least 11 different types of fog.

Since snow muffles sound, the thunder during a thundersnow storm can only be heard for a few miles.

The Yangtze River floods in China during the summer of 1931 made for the worst natural disaster in world history.

Every year, there are an estimated 16 million thunderstorms worldwide.

Clouds can travel faster than a cheetah can run.

Usually tornadoes are gray or white, but the debris they pick up can change their color.

One of the strongest winds ever recorded on our planet was 253 miles an hour (407 kmh). It was clocked on Barrow Island in Australia in 1996.

Wildfires cause some pinecones to open and sprout seeds.

There are more than 3 million flashes of lightning a day around the world.

Sandstorms can produce clouds of dirt and dust so large that they block the sun's light.

Wet 'n' Wild

50 Totally Random Facts About the RAIN FOREST

Scientists believe that rain forests are Earth's oldest living ecosystem.

Rain forests are home to more than half of the world's plant and animal species.

Some rain forest flowers look like insects so they can hide from hungry predators.

Some snakes that live in rain forests can glide through the air.

long-nosed potoroo

Some rain forest butterflies are so vibrant that they can be spotted from an airplane.

In the rain forest, some flowers can grow as big as small trees.

Tropical rain forests cover less than 3 percent of Earth's surface.

The world's oldest tropical rain forest, in Australia, has been around for more than 180 million years.

Rain forests are disappearing because of what's called deforestation, or the cutting down of a wide area of trees.

Rain forests are found on every continent except Antarctica.

The long-nosed potoroo is a small, furry mammal that lives in Australian rain forests. It has a snout that is longer than its hind foot!

A rain forest can have up to 25 times as many types of trees as other forests.

In a rain forest, you could walk for three minutes and not see the same kind of tree twice.

Jaguar

Strawberry poison dart frogs sometimes wrestle for up to 20 minutes.

Some piranhas, known for their razor-sharp teeth, don't actually eat meat.

The rain forest is so thick with leaves, it might rain for 10 minutes before any rain reaches the forest floor.

Rain forests get up to 400 inches (1,015 cm) of rain a year. New York City gets about 47 inches (119 cm).

Covering an area of land nearly as big as the 48 contiguous United States, South America's Amazon rain forest is the world's largest rain forest.

Piranhas

One of the biggest threats to rain forests and the planet is the clearing of trees for farming.

The Chimbu people in New Guinea grow sweet potatoes, bananas, and beans in rain forest gardens.

A fourth of the ingredients in modern medicines come from rain forest plants.

Up to 80 percent of the plants in Australian rain forests are not found anywhere else in the world.

Jaguars are nighttime hunters that eat 85 different kinds of prey, including iguanas, armadillos, and deer.

Rain forests help combat climate change by absorbing carbon dioxide.

There are two different types of rain forest: Tropical rain forests are near the equator, where it is warmest, and temperate rain forests are found in cooler areas.

Most rain forest animals live in trees.

The rain forest has four layers: the emergent layer at the top, the canopy, the understory, and the forest floor.

Trees in the rain forest can grow as tall as 200 feet (61 m)—the height of a 20-story building.

Less than 2 percent of sunlight reaches the hot, damp rain forest floor, where dead plants help bacteria thrive.

THE RHINOCEROS HORNBILL BIRD GETS ITS NAME FROM THE HORNLIKE STRUCTURE ON ITS HEAD.

Small rodents called pygmy gliders, found in Australian rain forests, glide from branch to branch using parachute-like flaps of skin between their legs.

Borneo is the third largest island in the world and was once mostly covered by rain forest. Today, more than 30 percent of the rain forest has been cut down for timber, paper, and to make room to grow crops.

Trees in the rain forest can be more than 1,000 years old.

Pineapples, cinnamon, cacao, and bananas all grow in rain forests.

More than a fifth of Earth's butterfly species can be found in South American rain forests.

Scarlet macaws

The red-bellied pacu, a kind of rain forest fish, can remove shells from nuts before eating them.

Armadillos that live in rain forests can hold their breath underwater for six minutes.

Capuchin monkeys poke each other's eyes to show friendship.

There are rainbow-colored grasshoppers in the Peruvian rain forest.

Okapis can be found only in the Ituri Rainforest in the Democratic Republic of the Congo.

Kinkajous use their long tongues to grab snacks from inside beehives.

Bridal veil stinkhorn mushroom

Almost 50 percent of the original rain forest land on our planet has been destroyed by human activity.

A rain forest mushroom called the bridal veil stinkhorn smells like rotting meat.

The largest rodent on Earth, the capybara, looks like a giant guinea pig.

Scarlet macaws—tropical parrots with brilliant red, blue, and yellow feathers—mate for life.

Poison dart frogs have bright colors to warn predators that they are toxic.

THE CALL OF A BLACK HOWLER MONKEY CAN BE HEARD UP TO 2 MILES (3 KM) AWAY.

Tropical rain forest vegetation →

Temperate rain forest

Green anacondas are one of the largest snakes in the world. They can weigh up to 550 pounds (250 kg) and grow as long as a school bus.

A mushroom found in the tropical rain forest of Ecuador can break down plastic.

Deforestation of tropical rain forests causes the same amount of carbon pollution as all the cars, buses, planes, and trains on Earth combined.

Deforestation of a tropical rain forest

Rock On!

88 Totally Random Facts About ROCKS and MINERALS

Rocks make up four of the planets in our solar system: **MERCURY, VENUS, EARTH,** and **MARS.**

Halite is the mineral we know as table salt.

Icebergs are considered minerals.

There are two types of igneous rocks: intrusive rocks, which form when magma solidifies belowground, and extrusive rocks, which are created by magma that has erupted onto Earth's surface as lava.

The Lincoln Memorial in Washington, D.C., is made of granite and marble, two types of rock.

Blackboards were first made of slate—a metamorphic rock.

The color of allochromatic minerals is due to flaws in their makeup.

Ancient Egyptians used copper, gold, and silver as mirrors.

Rocks have been around for 4.55 billion years.

Earth's crust is made of rock.

Minerals are made up of chemical elements like iron, gold, hydrogen, and oxygen.

Geologists group rocks into three major categories: igneous, sedimentary, and metamorphic.

Some minerals also glow under ultraviolet light.

Buildings in the ancient city of Petra, Jordan, are carved out of sandstone.

Sedimentary rock is formed by water and wind.

Minerals make up 6 percent of the human body.

The Egyptian Pyramids at Giza were built using rocks containing the remains of tiny sea creatures.

The top of Devils Tower is flat. It covers an area of 1.5 acres (0.6 ha).

Devils Tower is located in Wyoming. The tower is made of igneous rock and formed into columns as magma cooled.

The area surrounding Devils Tower is home to prairie dogs, which are ground squirrels that live together in large groups.

A movie poster from *Close Encounters of the Third Kind* features Devils Tower.

We are not alone
CLOSE ENCOUNTERS
OF THE THIRD KIND

Falling meteorites

Stonehenge

About 4,500 years ago, humans moved giant bluestones up to 180 miles (290 km) to create Stonehenge. How they did it remains a mystery.

Rocks from space that fall to Earth are called meteorites.

Rock shapes Earth's highest mountains and deepest oceans.

There are over 4,000 minerals.

Most of the rock that is exposed on Earth's surface is sedimentary rock.

Sedimentary rock is made up of layers of sand, mud, and crushed stones.

The mineral salt was so precious in ancient times that it was considered as valuable as gold.

Some Native Americans believed turquoise could bring rain during times of drought.

Talc is the softest mineral on Earth. It's soft enough to be scratched with a fingernail.

Minerals are categorized into three types by color: idiochromatic, allochromatic, and pseudochromatic.

Idiochromatic minerals have consistent colors based solely on their makeup.

Some rocks, called ores, have gold or silver on and inside them.

The hardest mineral is diamond.

A sedimentary rock known as flint was used in prehistoric times to make tools such as arrowheads and knives.

Rocks are made up of one or more minerals.

Rubies are rarer than emeralds or diamonds.

Glacier

A ruby

Peanut Butter Can Be Converted into a Diamond!

IN A QUEST TO LEARN MORE ABOUT HOW OUR PLANET FORMED, GERMAN SCIENTIST DAN FROST ACCIDENTALLY DISCOVERED A WAY TO TURN PEANUT BUTTER INTO DIAMONDS. Earth is like a big, rocky onion made up of three layers: the crust, mantle, and core. **Frost was studying these layers and working to copy the crystal-like rocks believed to exist in Earth's lower mantle.** During his research, he discovered an effect that might pull carbon dioxide from the crust down into deeper layers. **The process removes oxygen from carbon dioxide, leaving behind the element carbon.** Under intense pressure, carbon can form diamonds. To copy this in the lab, Frost tried applying these high pressures to a carbon-rich material. Then he thought, "Hey, why not peanut butter?" **The chemical hydrogen entered the mix and ruined the experiment, but not before diamonds emerged in the high-pressure environment. Now that really rocks!**

Fulgurite is a glassy rock that's created when lightning strikes beach sand.

The presidents' heads at Mount Rushmore were carved from an igneous rock called granite.

A mineral called painite is one of the rarest gemstones in the world.

A rock is formed when two or more minerals come together.

Quartz makes up 12 percent of Earth's land and 20 percent of our planet's crust.

Some mineral crystals are so tiny you need a microscope to see them.

The mineral feldspar covers about 60 percent of Earth's crust.

Rocks are in everyday things, like soap, toothpaste, and batteries.

Graphite is a mineral that's used in pencils.

JADE WAS HIGHLY PRIZED IN ANCIENT CHINA. IT WAS CONSIDERED A SYMBOL OF PURITY.

carving of a dragon made of jade

Some of the moai statues on Rapa Nui (Easter Island)

Easter Island, also known as Rapa Nui, is home to almost 900 giant stone figures known as moai. These statues were carved from hardened volcanic ash hundreds of years ago.

Uluru in Australia is the biggest monolith, or single standing block of rock, on Earth. It is over 1,142 feet (348 m) tall.

The most common mineral on Earth is bridgmanite, which makes up 38 percent of the planet as a whole.

The Hope Diamond is a rare blue diamond.

Sedimentary rocks are often found near oceans and lakes, or areas that once had oceans and lakes.

Fossils can often be found in sedimentary rocks.

Metamorphic rocks are formed deep within Earth.

The word *mineral* comes from a Latin word that means "something mined."

There is a salt mine in Ohio that runs underneath Lake Erie.

Earth's core is so hot that it can melt rock.

Obsidian, a naturally sharp mineral, was used by the Aztecs to make their weapons.

Some rocks in the Grand Canyon are almost 2 billion years old.

Fireworks contain minerals such as sodium, which makes yellows; barium, which gives off a green color; and copper, which makes blues.

Minerals are solid substances made of one or more elements that form naturally on our planet.

Some of the minerals in Saturn's rings are the size of buses.

Stalactites and stalagmites are mineral formations found in caves. Stalactites hang down from a cave's ceiling, like icicles. Stalagmites grow up from the cave floor.

Uluru is located in Australia's Northern Territory in the arid "Red Centre."

The most expensive type of gemstone is a blue diamond, which can cost as much as $3.93 million per carat (0.2 g).

Gypsum is a calcium-rich mineral used to BAKE CAKES.

Medieval painters used the mineral cinnabar for the bright red pigment it produces.

Although we may not see it, natural forces like earthquakes, water, wind, heat, and cold continuously recycle rock.

Silicate minerals make up around 90 percent of Earth's crust.

Fossils are the remains of plants and animals that have turned into rock over thousands, if not millions, of years.

The color of pseudochromatic minerals can appear to change depending on where light hits them.

A German scientist named Friedrich Mohs created the Mohs hardness scale in 1812. It is used to identify minerals by testing their hardness.

Pumice is the only rock that can float on water.

Heating coal in water creates steam that moves turbines to make electricity.

Geologists are scientists who study rocks.

Diamonds come in many colors, including blue, yellow, orange, red, green, and black.

Metamorphic rocks are formed when sedimentary and igneous rocks have been changed by heat and pressure.

Quartz crystals can produce electricity.

In the 1960s, a human-made ruby was used to create the first laser.

Scientists think it rains diamonds on Neptune and Saturn.

Pearls, made of the mineral aragonite, are the only gemstones made by living creatures.

Peridot has been found in meteorites.

The world's biggest crystals grow in Mexico's Cave of the Crystals, with some 36.1 feet (11 m) long and 3.3 feet (1 m) wide.

A crystal is formed when mineral particles are arranged in a repeating pattern.

One legend says wearing an opal could make a person invisible.

Humans started using rocks as tools more than 2.6 million years ago.

Ancient Egyptians believed topaz's warm glow came from the sun god Ra.

Fluorite is a mineral used in telescopes and camera lenses.

The 104-carat Stuart Sapphire is featured on the United Kingdom's Imperial State Crown.

The Stuart Sapphire

THE HOT LIQUID INSIDE A VOLCANO IS CALLED MAGMA. ONCE MAGMA ERUPTS FROM THE VOLCANO, IT'S CALLED LAVA.

Amazing Erupters

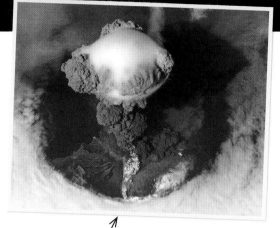

Eruption of Sarychev volcano, Pacific Ocean, seen from the International Space Station

30 Totally Random Facts About VOLCANOES

Twelve U.S. states have active volcanoes. Of these, Alaska has the most. • **When dinosaurs roamed Earth, there were active volcanoes on the moon.** • A restaurant on the island of Lanzarote, part of the Canary Islands, cooks its food using the heat of a volcano. • **Some glaciers contain volcanoes.** • Diamonds have been thrust to Earth's surface through volcanic eruptions. • **There are volcanoes in space.** • Olympus Mons, a volcano on Mars, is 80 times taller than the Eiffel Tower and the largest volcano in our solar system. • **An erupting volcano can cause lightning strikes.** • Mount Etna, located on the Italian island of Sicily, is the most active volcano in Europe. • **In 2010, huge amounts of ash spewing from a volcanic eruption in Iceland stopped air travel across Europe for seven days.** • Jupiter's moon Io is the most volcanically active place in our solar system. • **The origin of the word *volcano* is from Vulcan, the Roman god of fire.** • Between 5 and 10 percent of people on Earth live in the "danger range" of a volcano. • **There are three types of volcanoes: active, dormant, and extinct.** • Venus has about 1,600 known volcanoes, more than any other planet in our solar system. • **Indonesia has more active volcanoes than any other country.** • Volcanoes are considered extinct if they have not erupted in at least 10,000 years and are not expected to erupt again. • **Volcanic eruptions on Earth can be seen from space.** • The fastest lava flow ever recorded traveled at about 40 miles an hour (64 kmh) when it erupted out of a volcano in central Africa in 1977. • **Mauna Loa in Hawaii is the largest active volcano in the world. It towers more than 13,000 feet (3,960 m).** • Hawaii's

El Diablo restaurant, Lanzarote

Mauna Kea volcano is the tallest mountain in the world at 33,500 feet (10,211 m) from its base under the ocean to its peak aboveground. • **An area known as the Ring of Fire contains more than 450 active volcanoes. It runs almost 25,000 miles (40,230 km) around the rim of the Pacific Ocean.** • There are about 1,500 active volcanoes on Earth. • **The lava and ash from volcanoes break down into rich and fertile soil, creating the perfect conditions for farming and plant life.** • Mount Vesuvius erupted in A.D. 79, destroying and burying the Italian city of Pompeii under a thick layer of ash and pumice, a type of volcanic rock. • **The biggest recorded eruption in recent history was Mount Tambora in 1815. It could be heard from 1,200 miles (1,930 km) away.** • The loudest sound ever recorded was the 1883 eruption of Krakatoa, a volcano in Southeast Asia. • **A huge magma chamber under Yellowstone National Park extends from 12 to 30 miles (19–48 km) underground.** • Volcanoes mostly form at the edges of tectonic plates, which are large slabs of rock that together make up Earth's crust.

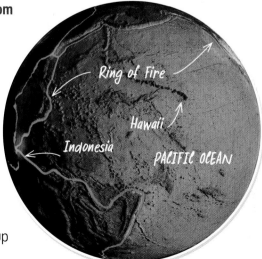

Ring of Fire

Hawaii

Indonesia

PACIFIC OCEAN

Out on a Limb

50 Totally Random Facts About FLOWERS and TREES

Bluebell flowers were once used to make glue.

Counting the rings inside a tree can reveal its age.

Hyperion, a redwood in California, is the world's tallest living tree at 380 feet (116 m).

El Árbol del Tule, a Montezuma cypress in Mexico, is the widest tree on Earth. It has a diameter of 38 feet (11.5 m) and measures 119 feet (36 m) around the trunk.

Mangrove trees grow along the shorelines of rivers and estuaries in tropical places around the world.

In India, the "Great Banyan tree" sprawls over an area of more than 3 acres (1 ha).

The Venus flytrap is a carnivorous, or meat-eating, plant. It eats insects, such as ants and grasshoppers, and arachnids such as spiders.

Venus flytrap with a trapped fly

Flowers of the lavender plant have been used as a perfume since ancient times.

The oldest flower ever discovered is *Montsechia vidalii*, an aquatic plant that lived about 130 million years ago.

Washington, D.C.'s cherry blossom trees were a gift from Japan. The trees were planted in 1912.

Sunflowers always face the sunlight, moving with the sun as it goes from east to west throughout the day.

Apples, strawberries, and peaches are in the same plant family as roses.

Trees take in water and nutrients through their roots. Roots also anchor a tree in place.

Conifers are a family of trees that produce cones. Some cones are male and others are female.

Water lilies can be found blooming on the surfaces of lakes and ponds. Their roots grow into the mud underneath.

Sunflowers can release toxic chemicals to keep other plants from getting too close to them.

Scientists think that trees can communicate with each other.

A grove of quaking aspen trees in Utah shares a root system that is about 80,000 years old.

African baobab tree

The African baobab tree can live for 2,000 years. Their trunks are so large that they are used as shelter by animals and even people.

The rare corpse flower doesn't bloom regularly like most flowers do. It only blooms when it has enough energy stored inside.

If you grow an apple tree from a seed, the new tree won't produce the same variety of apples as the tree that the seed came from.

In the 1600s, tulips were more valuable than gold.

The bark of a giant sequoia tree can be up to 2 feet (61 cm) thick at the base.

The flower with the world's largest bloom is the *Rafflesia arnoldii*, which can stretch 3 feet (1 m) across and weigh up to 15 pounds (7 kg).

Scientists think flowers first appeared on Earth between **140 AND 250 MILLION YEARS AGO.**

Bleeding heart plants get their name from the heart-shaped flowers they produce. Bleeding hearts are also fire resistant.

Trees spread their seeds with the wind, or through animals that eat the tree's fruit and drop the seeds in new places.

The queen of the night cactus flower only blooms at night. By morning the flowers close.

Maple syrup comes from the sap of the sugar maple tree.

The coco de mer palm tree only grows in the Seychelles, an island nation in the Indian Ocean. These trees grow seeds that can weigh up to 55 pounds (25 kg) each, the largest seed of any plant.

Mangroves are the only trees in the world that can grow in salt water.

Ancient fossil forests have been found in Antarctica.

The underwater roots of mangrove trees provide safe places for young fish to hide from predators.

Methuselah, a bristlecone pine, is the oldest tree on Earth, with an estimated age of about 4,800 years.

Tree trunks transport nutrients up from a tree's roots.

The shape and coloring of a bird of paradise flower look just like what you'd see on a tropical bird.

about five million dollars to develop. It is now one of the most expensive flowers in the world.

If you touch the *Mimosa pudica*, also known as the sensitive plant, it will respond by folding up its leaves.

Rose petals are edible.

According to scientists, there are more than **THREE TRILLION TREES ON EARTH.**

Mangrove tree

A bristlecone pine

Bird of paradise flower

Rafflesia arnoldii (corpse flower)

When a corpse flower blooms, it only blooms for 24 to 36 hours, and it smells like rotting flesh.

There are only 1,000 corpse flowers left in the wild. It is considered an endangered plant species.

The canopy of a monkey pod tree can spread about 100 to 200 feet (30–61 m) wide.

The orchid mantis is a species of praying mantis that looks just like an actual orchid flower.

The Power of Trees

- Trees improve air quality by removing pollution from the atmosphere.

- **One large tree provides a one-day supply of oxygen for up to four people.**

- Trees planted along the road can reduce air pollution inside people's homes by more than 50 percent.

- **Areas shaded by trees can have temperatures more than 20 degrees lower than unshaded areas.**

- Trees help combat global warming by absorbing and storing carbon dioxide, and replacing it with fresh oxygen.

- **One acre (0.4 ha) of trees absorbs the same amount of carbon dioxide that a car produces after being driven 26,000 miles (42,840 km).**

WATER IS REFERRED TO AS H₂O because it's made up of two hydrogen (H) atoms and one oxygen (O) atom.

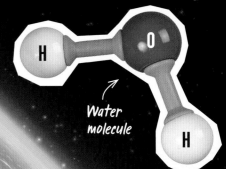

Water molecule

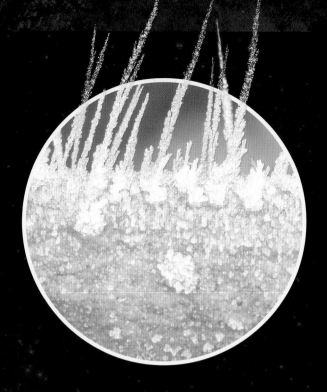

A Blue World

98 Totally Random Facts About *WATER*

Water is in all living things.

Life on Earth would not be possible without water.

Water can freeze upward to form ice spikes.

Less than one percent of Earth's water is usable for drinking, farming, and making things.

Water helps protect our planet from getting too hot or cold.

A person can live about four times longer without food than without water.

The West African lungfish can survive in dried mud puddles for up to four years.

Daily, the average American uses about 82 gallons (310 L) of water.

Male sandgrouse birds store water in their feathers by wading in watering holes until their feathers soak in the liquid. They then take the water back for their chicks to drink.

Water expands when it freezes.

Scientists who search for life on other planets look for water first.

Oceans contain about 97 percent of Earth's water.

Oceans cover about 71 percent of our planet.

About 0.001 percent of Earth's water is always hovering in our atmosphere.

If all the water in the atmosphere was released at once, an inch (2.5 cm) of rain would drench the planet.

Only 3.5 percent of Earth's water is freshwater, free of salt.

Freshwater can be found in lakes, streams, and rivers.

Over 68 percent of Earth's freshwater is frozen in glaciers.

About 30 percent of Earth's freshwater is underground.

There is about 4.5 ounces (128 g) of salt in every gallon (3.8 L) of ocean water.

The kangaroo rat can survive without water for almost its entire life, which is usually about 10 years.

The saltiest body of water in the world is the Don Juan Pond in Antarctica.

Thousands of bacteria, viruses, and microscopic fish can live in a single drop of ocean water.

Even though a tree seems solid, more than half of it is water.

Angel oak tree

TEN PERCENT OF HOMES HAVE LEAKS THAT WASTE 90 GALLONS (341 L) OR MORE PER DAY.

Some of Earth's water may have come from comets from outer space.

Comets are mostly made up of ice.

Ice floats because it is less dense than water.

The human body uses water for almost everything it does.

Water works like bubble wrap in our bodies, acting as a natural shock absorber.

Water has a unique stickiness that makes it form droplets.

Water's stickiness helps plants suck it up through their internal straws.

Turning off the faucet while you brush your teeth can save 8 gallons (30 L) of water a day.

It takes 11 gallons (42 L) of water to make one slice of white bread.

Desert tortoises can store 40 percent of their body weight in water in their bladders.

One gallon (3.8 L) of water weighs about 8 pounds (3.5 kg).

A leaky toilet can waste more than 22,000 gallons (83,280 L) of water a year. That's enough to take three baths every day.

An eight-minute shower uses about 40 gallons (151 L) of water.

Water cannot be squeezed. If you try to compress it, it squirts out.

In the United States, 80 percent of water is used for irrigation and to cool electric power plants.

There are 326 million cubic miles (1.36 billion cu km) of water on the planet.

If the world's water supply filled half a bathtub, only about a half teaspoon (2.5 ml) of that would be usable.

NASA has discovered water in the form of ice on the moon.

A 2.6-billion-year-old pocket of water was discovered in a Canadian mine.

More than 2,000 gallons (7,570 L) of water are needed to produce 1 pound (0.5 kg) of chocolate.

The soil on Mars contains liquid water.

The average household's leaks can waste the same amount of water it takes to wash 270 loads of laundry.

More than a trillion gallons (3.78 trillion L) of water are wasted annually. That's enough to supply water to more than 11 million homes.

The body of an adult human is made up of about 60 percent water.

The largest tsunami wave ever recorded was more that 1,700 feet (518 m) tall, which is about as high as a 160-story building!

In Iceland, 30 percent of the electricity comes from steam.

The Blue Lagoon in Iceland formed from water coming out of a geothermal plant. The plant is also what keeps the water a warm 92°F to 100°F (33°C–38°C).

Hot water and cold water sound different when you pour them.

Some animals, including insects, can "walk" on water.

Plasma, which makes up more than half the volume of our blood, is about 90 percent water.

The Puerto Princesa Subterranean River is an underground river that's part of a cave system in the Philippines. The river flows directly into the sea.

The human body is best adapted to live at sea level.

Water dissolves more substances than any other liquid.

Headaches, muscle cramps, and scratchy eyes are all signs you're not drinking enough water.

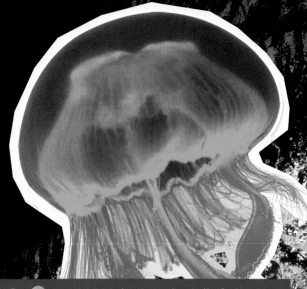

A cucumber and a jellyfish are both about **95 PERCENT WATER.**

Pond skaters

THAT'S SO RANDOM:

You Drink the Same Water as Cleopatra, George Washington, and Even *T. rex* Once Did!

FROM THE BEGINNING OF TIME, EARTH HAS HAD A FINITE AMOUNT OF WATER. THAT MEANS THE WATER NEVER REALLY GOES AWAY, ALTHOUGH IT MAY CHANGE FORM. You are drinking the same water that your great-great-great-great-grandparents drank. And one day, your great-great-great-great-great-grandchildren will drink the water that you are drinking today. **As strange as it sounds, the water in your glass will still be here in 30 million years.** Why doesn't the supply run out or evaporate? The answer is that water is constantly recycled through Earth's system in a process called the water cycle. The water cycle is the path that all water follows as it moves around the planet in its different states. Water in its liquid form is found in oceans, rivers, lakes—and even underground. **Solid ice is found in glaciers, snow, and at the North and South Poles.** Water vapor—a gas—is found in Earth's atmosphere. **The path that water takes includes many processes that circulate water through Earth's subsystems.** For example, water evaporates from within soils and from oceans and lakes. This evaporated water accumulates as water in clouds. Then that same water falls directly back to Earth as rain or snow. **The rainwater replenishes the oceans and lakes and is soaked up by trees and vegetation, and the whole cycle repeats itself.** Ponder that the next time you brush your teeth!

Water transports chemicals, nutrients, and minerals through our bodies and also through our planet.

Water is the only substance on Earth that is found naturally as a liquid, a solid, and a gas.

It takes longer to boil an egg in the mountains than it does at sea level.

Water is measured by volume.

Some beetles that live in the Namib Desert in southern Africa collect water from fog to drink.

Scientists estimate there are 1 million animal species living in our oceans.

It's estimated that only 5 percent of the world's oceans has been explored.

There are 38,000 different kinds of microbes in 4 cups (1 L) of seawater.

Water is the second most abundant substance in the universe.

In the last 100 years, water use has grown at more than twice the rate of our population.

Ticks and mites can absorb water from the air without drinking.

It takes 48 gallons (182 L) of water to make 1 cup (237 ml) of milk.

IN THE DEEP OCEAN, GIANT TSUNAMI WAVES CAN TRAVEL FASTER THAN AIRPLANES, AT 500 MILES AN HOUR (805 KMH).

Scientists estimate that millions of species of ocean critters have yet to be discovered.

Throwing boiling water into cold air can make snow.

If the ice that covers Antarctica were to melt, it would raise the level of the oceans by about 200 feet (61 m).

The water-holding frog in Australia can live for years without water. **It burrows in the sand, enclosing itself in a cocoon, and eats its own skin.**

Only three people have ever explored Challenger Deep, the deepest part of the ocean.

The thorny devil, a kind of lizard, traps water in its scales, then transports it to its mouth under its skin.

Cows can consume up to 100 gallons (378 L) of water a day.

Washing dishes for three meals takes about 10 gallons (38 L) of water.

A typical camel can drink 53 gallons (200 L) of water in three minutes.

Aquifers are areas of porous rock soaked with groundwater. Water from precipitation, such as rain or snow, moves through the aquifer and comes back out through wells and springs.

Shortening your shower by four minutes can save up to 20 gallons (75 L) of water.

It takes more than 2,000 gallons (7,570 L) of water to make a pair of jeans.

Water is heavier than air.

In some countries, more people have cell phones than working toilets.

A koala will lick rain as it runs down a tree trunk. They also get water from the eucalyptus leaves they eat.

Water isn't clear; it's slightly blue.

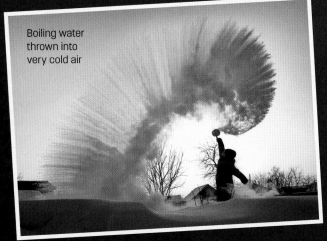

Boiling water thrown into very cold air

 It takes about 630 gallons (2,385 L) of water to make one **ONE HAMBURGER.**

The largest known water mass in our universe is 12 billion light-years away.

The Atlantic Ocean is saltier than the Pacific Ocean.

Sound travels four times faster underwater.

Scientists discovered water beyond Earth in 1969.

Some cities buy or import water from other places.

The Pacific Ocean is Earth's largest body of water. It covers more than a third of the planet's surface.

Lake Baikal is the deepest lake in the world. It's also the largest freshwater lake on Earth by volume, or the amount of space the water takes up.

Lake Baikal, Russia

126 Totally Random Facts About

Happening History

A Look Back in Time

History Makers

Rosa Parks

48 Totally Random Facts About WOMEN WHO CHANGED THE WORLD

Rosa Parks is known as the mother of the civil rights movement for refusing to give up her bus seat to a white person in Montgomery, Alabama, U.S.A., in 1955.

Michelle Obama was the first African American First Lady of the United States. As First Lady, she led many important initiatives, including a global campaign to encourage kids to eat well and exercise.

Florence Nightingale is credited with being the founder of modern nursing.

Margaret Thatcher was the United Kingdom's first female prime minister. Known as the Iron Lady, Thatcher proved that women could be strong leaders.

Primatologist Jane Goodall has led the world's longest running continuous wildlife research project with chimpanzees. Her unique connection with chimps has inspired people to help protect them.

Hillary Clinton made history in the United States as the first female presidential nominee of a major party in 2016.

Elizabeth Blackwell was the first woman to receive a medical degree in the United States in 1849, inspiring other women to pursue careers in medicine.

Anne Frank changed the world by leaving a diary of what her life was like while she and her family were hiding from the Nazis during the Holocaust.

In the 1960s and 1970s, journalist Gloria Steinem was at the forefront of the feminist movement, which fought for equal rights and treatment for women. She continues her activism today.

Mother Teresa spent her lifetime caring for the world's poorest and sickest people and became a role model for sacrifice, strength, and kindness.

England's Queen Elizabeth II is the longest-reigning queen and female head of state in the world.

Oprah Winfrey is known for her long-running talk show, which ran for 25 years, and her worldwide philanthropy. In 2003, she became a billionaire, one of only two African American female billionaires at the time.

Cleopatra was ancient Egypt's last pharaoh.

SUSAN B. ANTHONY'S WORK FIGHTING FOR WOMEN'S RIGHTS IN THE MID-19TH CENTURY LED TO THE 19TH AMENDMENT, WHICH GIVES WOMEN THE RIGHT TO VOTE.

Mural of Anne Frank in Amsterdam, the Netherlands

In 2009, Associate Justice Sonia Sotomayor became the third woman sworn in to serve on the U.S. Supreme Court. She is the first woman of color and first Latina to serve on the court.

Eleanor Roosevelt was the longest-serving First Lady, during her husband's four terms in the White House from 1933 to 1945. She was a strong supporter of the civil rights movement.

Sojourner Truth escaped slavery in 1826, after which she became a women's rights activist, spending her life fighting for equality and justice.

Born in Massachusetts in 1830, Emily Dickinson learned to read and write at a time when women weren't supposed to. She went on to become one of the greatest American poets of all time.

Lucille Ball was the first woman to run a television studio. Her comedy show, *I Love Lucy*, had fans all over the world.

Sojourner Truth Monument, Battle Creek, MI, U.S.A.

EIGHTEEN-TIME GRAMMY AWARD–WINNING SINGER ARETHA FRANKLIN WAS KNOWN AS THE QUEEN OF SOUL FOR HER INCREDIBLE SINGING ABILITY.

Nancy Pelosi was the first female to serve as Speaker in the U.S. House of Representatives.

Ruby Bridges was six years old when she became the first African American student to integrate into an all-white school—a result of the *Brown v. Board of Education* Supreme Court case, which outlawed public school segregation.

In 1976, Barbara Walters became the first woman to coanchor the evening news on a major network, ABC.

Jane Austen wrote about 18th-century British life in her popular and widely read books, including *Pride and Prejudice*, *Sense and Sensibility*, and *Emma*.

Helen Keller was the first deaf and blind person to earn a college degree, proving that anything is possible.

Human rights activist Malala Yousafzai was shot by a Taliban gunman at age 15. Not only did she survive to fight for female education, but at age 17 she became the youngest person ever to receive the Nobel Peace Prize.

Helen Keller on the Alabama state quarter

Polish physicist Marie Curie pioneered research on radioactivity and was the first woman to receive a Nobel Prize. She went on to win a second Nobel Prize, too.

Maya Angelou was an activist, poet, and author who worked alongside civil rights leaders Martin Luther King Jr. and Malcolm X to fight for racial justice and equality.

Madeleine Albright was the first female to be appointed U.S. secretary of state in 1997.

Indira Gandhi was the first woman to serve as the prime minister of India.

One of Mexico's greatest artists, Frida Kahlo created important paintings that explored topics of gender, class, and race.

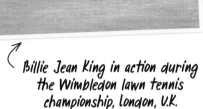

Billie Jean King in action during the Wimbledon lawn tennis championship, London, U.K.

Billie Jean King became the world's number one tennis player after winning an impressive 39 Grand Slam titles.

Japanese mountaineer Junko Tabei is the first female to climb the Seven Summits, a collective of the highest mountain on each continent.

Gymnast Nadia Comaneci is one of the youngest Olympic gold medalists in history and was the first person to receive a perfect score of 10 in Olympic gymnastics.

Malala Yousafzai wins the Nobel Peace Prize.

Portrait of Frida Kahlo drawn by a pavement artist in Mexico City, Mexico

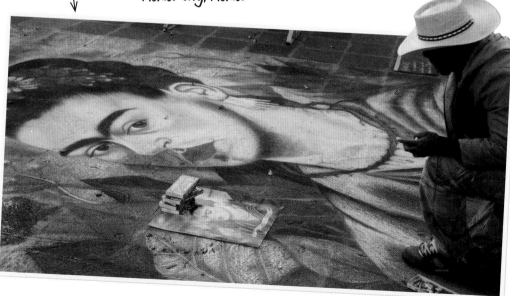

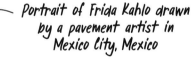

Astronaut Sally Ride on board the space shuttle Challenger

In 1968, Shirley Chisholm became the first African American woman elected to Congress. She represented New York's 12th Congressional District.

Corazon Aquino was the first female president of the Philippines. She brought democracy back to her country after a long period of dictatorship.

Dorothy Levitt was the first British female race car driver, proving women can have a need for speed.

Thirty-two-year-old Sally Ride was the first American woman to go to space, and one of the youngest astronauts ever.

Gertrude Ederle became the first woman to swim the English Channel in 1926, beating the men's record by two hours.

Clara Barton founded the American Red Cross in 1881. The Red Cross provides emergency assistance to people all over the world.

In 1981, Associate Justice Sandra Day O'Connor became the first woman to serve on the U.S. Supreme Court.

Kamala Harris made history as the first female and first woman of color to be elected vice president of the United States.

Born into slavery around 1820 in the United States, Harriet Tubman helped more than 70 enslaved people reach freedom through the Underground Railroad.

Barbara Jordan became the first southern African American woman to be elected to the U.S. House of Representatives in 1972. She represented Texas.

Pakistani leader Benazir Bhutto was the first woman to serve as prime minister of any Muslim-majority nation.

Ruth Bader Ginsburg was the second appointed female associate justice of the U.S. Supreme Court. She was a staunch advocate for women's rights.

Harper Lee changed the world with her Pulitzer Prize–winning classic *To Kill a Mockingbird*, which shed light on race and class injustices during the 1930s.

MORE THAN 100 YEARS BEFORE COMPUTERS, ADA LOVELACE'S MATHEMATICAL ENGINEERING SKILLS EARNED HER THE TITLE OF THE "FIRST COMPUTER PROGRAMMER."

Game Changers

Alexander the Great →

48 Totally Random Facts About MEN WHO CHANGED THE WORLD

In addition to being an inventor and one of America's Founding Fathers, Benjamin Franklin was also a member of the International Swimming Hall of Fame.

It took four years for Michelangelo to complete his paintings on the ceiling of the Sistine Chapel. He built special platforms attached to the chapel's walls to help him reach above his head.

Mikhail Gorbachev, former leader of the Soviet Union, won a Nobel Peace Prize for his role in ending the Cold War with the United States. He led his country's transition to democracy.

As a young man, Abraham Lincoln was a wrestler who was honored in the National Wrestling Hall of Fame. As president of the United States, Lincoln created policies that would end slavery across the country.

Alexander the Great was a military commander and king of ancient Greece. During his reign, he conquered land from Asia to Europe.

Artist Pablo Picasso was once accused of stealing the *Mona Lisa*, a crime he didn't commit.

William Shakespeare, considered one of the most talented writers of all time, penned plays, including *Romeo and Juliet* and *Macbeth*. He even wrote a curse for his grave, to keep robbers away.

CIVIL RIGHTS ICON MARTIN LUTHER KING JR. FOUGHT FOR RACIAL EQUALITY IN THE 1960s, SPEAKING ABOUT NONVIOLENCE AND INSPIRING SOCIAL CHANGE.

Frederick Douglass statue, Easton, MD, U.S.A.

Frederick Douglass disguised himself as a sailor to escape from slavery. He went on to speak and write books that would inspire others to fight for freedom.

Socrates, an ancient Greek philosopher, believed in questioning everything to understand it better. He is known as the father of Western philosophy.

Indian leader Mahatma Gandhi believed in nonviolence. He led the way to India's independence from British rule.

Winston Churchill, Great Britain's prime minister during World War II, was known to be very accident prone. He fell from horses, got hit by a car in New York City when he looked the wrong way, and nearly drowned in a lake.

In 1977, American politician Harvey Milk became a trailblazer for the LGBTQ community as one of the country's first openly gay elected officials.

At age 11, Austrian composer Wolfgang Amadeus Mozart wrote his first opera. But music wasn't his only love. So were animals. There is even a Haitian frog species named after him. It's called: *Eleutherodactylus amadeus*.

Neil Armstrong

American astronaut Neil Armstrong was the first person to ever step foot on the moon. More than half a billion people watched the event on television.

In 1776, Founding Father Thomas Jefferson authored the Declaration of Independence. Later as the third U.S. president, he doubled the country's size with the Louisiana Purchase. Jefferson also had many interests, including being a fossil collector.

American activist Cesar Chavez organized communities to fight for better working conditions for migrant farmworkers in the United States.

Ancient Greek philosopher Plato started the first university, called The Academy, which taught students about human nature.

Thomas Paine was an influential writer who wrote the best-selling pamphlet *Common Sense*, which motivated American people to seek independence from Great Britain.

Wolfgang Amadeus Mozart, aged 13

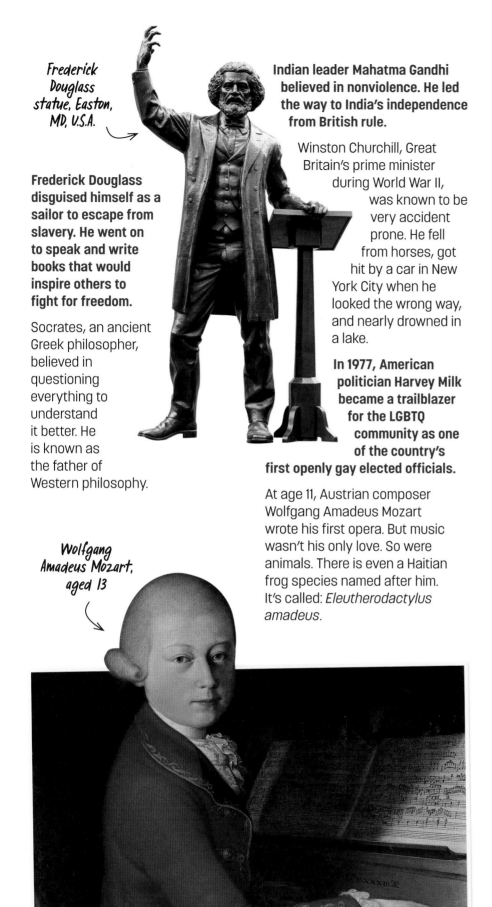

NICOLAUS COPERNICUS WAS A POLISH SCIENTIST AND MATHEMATICIAN WHO CAME UP WITH THE IDEA THAT THE SUN IS AT THE CENTER OF THE SOLAR SYSTEM AND THAT THE PLANETS ORBIT AROUND IT. HE ALSO HAS AN ELEMENT NAMED AFTER HIM—COPERNICIUM.

Marco Polo was an Italian explorer who made groundbreaking journeys to Asia and China.

Thomas Edison was an American inventor and businessman who helped introduce electric lightbulbs and the motion picture camera to the world. One of his lesser-known inventions was a series of talking dolls, which were a flop.

The Dalai Lama is the leader of the main branch of Buddhism. In his home of Tibet, he has worked to find peaceful ways to stand against China's rule over the region.

The Dalai Lama

Naturalist Charles Darwin came up with the idea of natural selection, which explains how species adapt to survive over time. For a period of time, Darwin's likeness appeared on the British 10-pound banknote.

Charles Darwin

Aristotle was both a philosopher and scientist in ancient Greece. He made discoveries in geometry, zoology, physics, astronomy, chemistry, and meteorology.

Known as the father of modern science, Galileo Galilei was the first person to study the cosmos through a telescope. His middle finger has been on display in several Italian museums.

George Washington only went to school until age 11. But he rose to become the first president of the United States. Washington was also a lover of dogs and gave his dogs names, including Sweet Lips and Madame Moose.

As a lawyer, Thurgood Marshall argued for school desegregation in front of the Supreme Court. He later became the first Black justice on the Supreme Court.

French chemist Louis Pasteur studied medicine and developed cures for rabies, anthrax, and other infectious diseases.

Nikola Tesla was a Serbian inventor and engineer who discovered important things about electric power. Today's Tesla cars are named after him.

World-famous scientist Albert Einstein made groundbreaking discoveries about light, matter, time, space, and gravity.

Tim Berners-Lee is a British computer scientist who invented the World Wide Web (WWW), which enables people to see websites on their computers. In 2004, he was knighted by Queen Elizabeth for his achievement.

Johann Sebastian Bach, a German composer of classical music, was considered one of the most talented composers of all time. He also wrote a jingle about coffee.

After watching an apple fall from a tree, English mathematician Sir Isaac Newton discovered the laws of gravity and motion.

Ancient Egyptian ruler Khufu ordered the building of the Great Pyramid at Giza, the oldest of the seven wonders of the ancient world.

Nelson Mandela was South Africa's first Black president. Under his leadership, he guided the country to becoming a multiracial democracy.

Brothers Orville and Wilbur Wright invented, constructed, and flew the world's first motor-operated airplane. The brothers tossed a coin to see who would fly first. Though Wilbur won, his attempt to fly was unsuccessful. When it was Orville's turn, he was able to become airborne, and so he became the first brother to fly.

Francis Bacon was an English philosopher and scientist known for creating the scientific method, which is a way to identify a problem, collect information, and test a solution.

Chinese inventor Cai Lun created the world's first paper using tree bark.

VENEZUELAN MILITARY AND POLITICAL LEADER SIMÓN BOLÍVAR LED THE REVOLUTION FOR SOUTH AMERICA'S INDEPENDENCE FROM SPAIN.

In 2008, Barack Obama was the first African American person to be elected president of the United States. He signed American taxpayer relief acts and ended military involvement in the Iraq War.

Leonardo da Vinci was both a painter and a scientist. His most famous paintings include the *Mona Lisa* and *The Last Supper*.

Bill Gates is an American businessman who led the computer revolution. He is also a writer and advocate in the fight against climate change.

President Barack Obama awards the Presidential Medal of Freedom to chemist Mario Molina.

Mexico-born Mario Molina was one of the first scientists to discover the environmental dangers of chlorofluorocarbons (CFCs), once commonly used in refrigerators and cleaning products. They are now banned in many parts of the world.

Muhammad Ali, known as one of the greatest boxers of all time, also starred in a Broadway show.

Dutch painter Rembrandt van Rijn was famous for painting people and capturing their moods on canvas. He liked dogs so much, he put them in some of his paintings.

Langston Hughes, an American poet and leader of the Harlem Renaissance, invented a style of poetry called "jazz poetry."

Leo Tolstoy was a Russian novelist and philosopher whose famous books include *War and Peace* and *Anna Karenina*.

The pyramids were built as tombs for pharaohs, leaders who ruled over ancient Egypt.

There are more than 130 pyramids in Egypt.

The Pyramids at Giza were built about 4,500 years ago.

The Great Pyramid of Giza is the largest pyramid in Egypt. Today it would cost billions of dollars to build.

King Tut was the youngest ruler of ancient Egypt. He became a pharaoh at age nine and ruled for 10 years before his death.

When archaeologists discovered King Tut's tomb in 1922, it had remained untouched for more than 3,000 years.

Although X-rays show King Tut had a broken leg that could have led to an infection and death, his death remains a mystery.

Scientists believe ancient Egyptians invented the very first "toothbrushes," made from twigs with brush-like ends of frayed wood.

Both Egyptian men and women wore makeup such as eyeliner.

The Egyptian alphabet was made up of hieroglyphs, pictures and symbols that represented words.

Ancient Egyptian police officers used dogs and even trained monkeys as service animals.

Ancient Egyptian believed their sun god, Ra, was reborn each morning with the rise of the sun.

Cats were so respected in ancient Egypt that wealthy owners would sometimes dress them in jewelry.

Tutankhamun hunting hippos with a harpoon on a reed boat

Great Pyramid of Giza

Secrets of the Tombs

30 Totally Random Facts About ANCIENT EGYPT

Hieroglyphs

Queen Nefertari playing senet

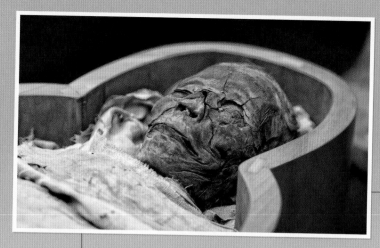

Cleopatra was a queen of Egypt, but she was not Egyptian; she was Greek.

The ancient Egyptian board game senet has been played for 5,000 years.

Ancient Egyptians invented a type of paper called papyrus, made from the papyrus plant that grew along the Nile River.

Ancient Egyptian women would have cones placed on their heads. The cones were scented and made of fat.

Sobekneferu was the first female ancient Egyptian pharaoh.

All of Egypt would be a desert without the Nile River. Less than 1 inch (2.5 cm) of rain falls throughout Egypt each year.

Hatshepsut ruled as pharaoh for 21 years, making her the longest-ruling female pharaoh of ancient Egypt.

Ancient Egyptians referred to their land as Kemet, which means "black land."

Toothpaste was invented by ancient Egyptians.

Ancient Egyptians shaved their eyebrows when their cats died as a sign of mourning.

Mummified pet cat

Magnificent Mummies

- The process of mummification took about 70 days.

- **The heart was the only organ left inside the body before a mummy was wrapped.**

- Pets in ancient Egypt were mummified and often buried with their owners.

- **Egyptian priests would open a mummy's mouth so that the person could speak and eat in the afterlife.**

- The bandages used for one mummy could stretch for nearly 1 mile (1.6 km).

- **Archaeologists in Egypt discovered mummies with golden tongues. They think these gold pieces were placed so that the dead could speak with Osiris, god of the underworld.**

Each stone block used to build the pyramids weighed **ALMOST 3 TONS (2.7 T).**

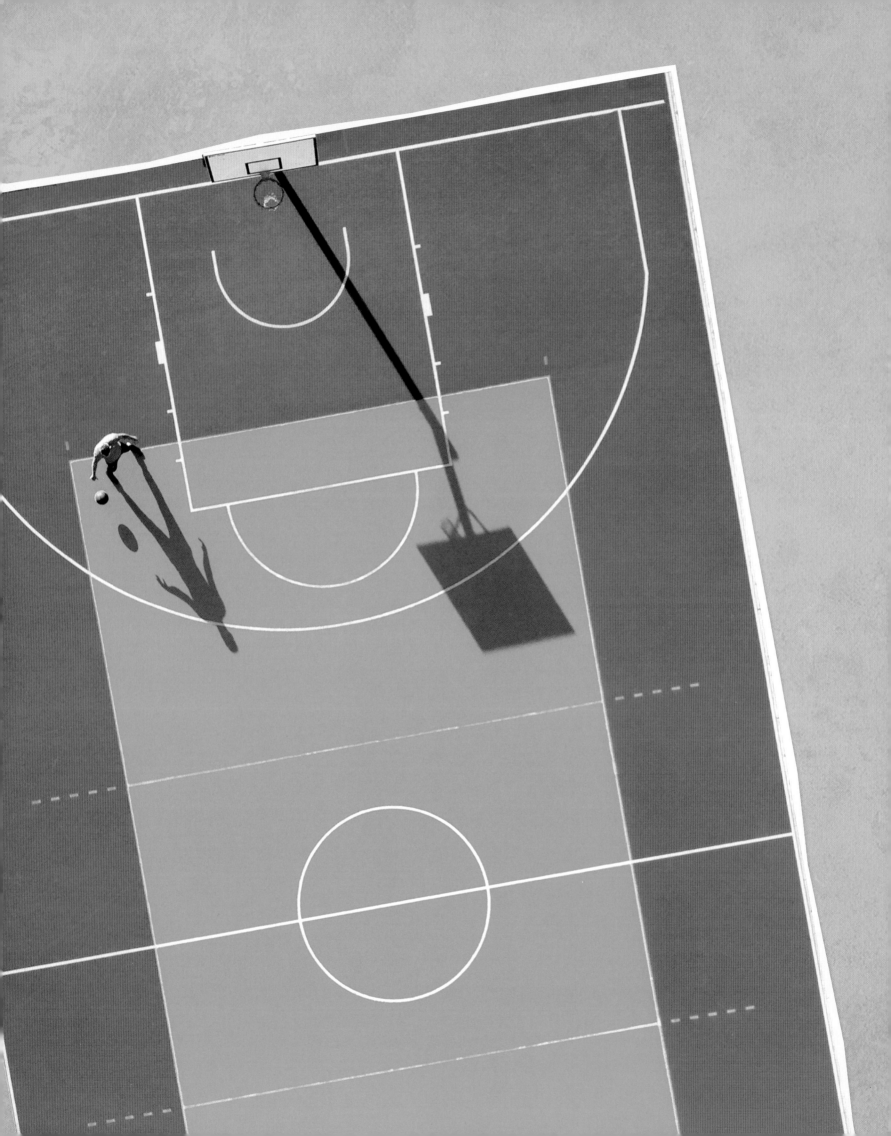

138 Totally Random Facts About

Splendid Sports

Swimming, Jumping, Running, and Racing

Going for the Gold

Statue of a Greek discus thrower

52 Totally Random Facts About the OLYMPICS

Usain Bolt of Jamaica, having run his last 100m race, pulls into his famous lighting bolt pose, London, U.K.

The Olympic Games are an international sporting event. The games switch between summer and winter sports every two years.

More than 200 countries participate in the Olympic Games.

The Summer Olympic Games cover 33 sports.

The first Olympic Games on record were held in ancient Greece in 776 B.C. They were held every four years until the fourth century A.D.

The modern Olympic Games started in 1896 in Athens, Greece.

Women were not allowed to compete in the Olympics until 1900.

The Olympic Games were canceled in 1916, 1940, and 1944 because of World War I and World War II.

The 2020 Summer Olympics in Tokyo, Japan, were postponed by a year because of the COVID-19 pandemic. Though they occurred in 2021, they were still called the 2020 Olympic Games.

Olympic athletes in first place get a gold medal; athletes coming in second get a silver medal; and third-place finishers, a bronze medal.

Chariot racing was an event at the early Olympic Games.

The opening ceremony of the 2008 Summer Olympics in Beijing, China

THE FIVE RINGS OF THE OLYMPIC SYMBOL REPRESENT THE FIVE PARTS OF THE WORLD THAT COMPETE: EUROPE, ASIA, AUSTRALIA, AFRICA, AND THE AMERICAS.

The Olympic Games stopped for 1,500 years because a Roman emperor banned them. He thought they were inconsistent with Christianity.

The 1908 Olympic Games lasted six months. Today, they last 16 days.

From 1924 to 1992, the Winter and Summer Olympics took place in the same year.

Only six athletes have won medals in both the Winter and Summer Olympics.

In the ancient Olympic Games, winners were given olive branch wreaths.

The official languages spoken at the Olympics are English, French, and the language of the host country.

From 1912 to 1948, painters, sculptors, writers, and musicians competed for Olympic medals.

When two Japanese pole-vaulters who were good friends won the event, they refused to vault against each other for second place. Judges awarded them the silver and bronze, which the athletes later cut and welded into two half-and-half medals.

The Olympic torch is lit in Greece using a special mirror and the sun's rays. It travels to the host city in a relay of runners, boats, airplanes, and canoes.

The Olympic torch has been to space.

Only one athlete has won medals for speed skating and cycling in the same year.

Hot-air ballooning and tug-of-war used to be Olympic sports.

The oldest athlete to take part in the Paralympics was Toshie Oi of Japan. At age 68, he participated as a discus thrower at the Rio Paralympics in 2016.

The six colors on the Olympic flag—blue, yellow, black, green, red, and the white background—were chosen because every country's flag uses at least one of them.

The first Winter Games were held in Chamonix, France, in 1924.

Gold medals were made of pure gold until 1912.

Today, the Olympics host city designs the medals for that year.

The tradition of awarding athletes with medals started in 1904.

It wasn't until 2012 that all countries sent female athletes to the Olympic Games.

Five thousand medals made from recycled electronic devices—including more than 6 million phones—were given at the Tokyo 2020 games.

THE FIRST PARALYMPICS WERE HELD IN ROME, ITALY, IN 1960. LIKE THE OLYMPICS, THE SUMMER AND WINTER PARALYMPICS EACH TAKE PLACE EVERY FOUR YEARS.

The ancient Olympic Games were held in honor of the Greek god Zeus. During the competitions, all wars had to stop.

Only five countries have been represented at every modern Summer Olympic Games: Greece, Great Britain, France, Switzerland, and Australia.

Medals for the 2016 Olympics in Rio de Janeiro, Brazil, were made with bits of leftover mirrors and X-ray plates, and the ribbons were made with recycled plastic from old bottles.

In the opening ceremony's Parade of Nations, Greece takes the lead and the host country goes last.

The youngest Olympian to ever compete was a 10-year-old Greek gymnast in 1896.

The United States has won more medals in the Summer Olympics than any other country, with a combined total of more than 2,600 medals.

Norway has won more medals in the Winter Olympic Games than any other country, with more than 350 medals.

South Korean male athletes who win an Olympic medal can skip their mandatory 18-month military service.

Australia melted down their one-cent and two-cent coins to make bronze medals for the 2000 Summer Olympics in Sydney.

Ireland won its first Olympic medal in 1924, for painting.

At the 1900 games in Paris, France, winners won paintings and works of art, as well as cups and trophies, instead of medals.

Gold, silver, and bronze medals represent time periods in Greek mythology.

The top eight athletes in each sport receive an Olympic diploma for participating.

The United States won gold in the wheelchair basketball games in the first Paralympics in 1960.

PARIS - LYON - MÉDITERRANÉE

CHAMONIX·MONT BLANC
TOUTES LES INSTALLATIONS DE SPORTS D'HIVER

A poster from the 1924 Chamonix Mont Blanc Winter Olympics

Tebogo Mofokeng of South Africa competing in the men's T62 400m final at the Tokyo 2020 Paralympic Games

Professional skateboarder Sky Brown of Great Britain competing at the 2021 summer Olympics in Japan. At 13, Brown became her country's youngest ever Olympic medalist when she won bronze in Tokyo.

Going for Gold

- **Ten gold medals from the 2014 Sochi Games contained pieces of meteorite.**

- Great Britain is the only country to win at least one gold medal at every Summer Games since the start of the modern Olympics.

- **A Ukrainian boxer auctioned off his gold medal for $1 million for charity. The person who bought it gave it back to the boxer.**

- In the 1920s, Johnny Weissmuller, the actor who later played Tarzan, won five gold medals for swimming.

- **Only one person has won gold medals at both the Summer and Winter Olympics. An American won in boxing and 12 years later in bobsledding.**

- The most decorated Olympian of all time is American swimmer Michael Phelps, who has won 23 gold, 3 silver, and 2 bronze medals. They were won across four Olympic Games, from Athens 2004 to Rio 2016.

Michael Phelps competes in the men's 200m individual medley at the Rio 2016 Summer Olympic Games.

THE TERM *SLAM DUNK* WAS COINED IN THE 1960s, BUT DUNK SHOTS HAVE BEEN AROUND SINCE THE 1930S.

Swish!

86 Totally Random Facts About BASKETBALL

Originally, basketball was played with a soccer ball.

Backboards were first put behind baskets to make sure spectators didn't touch the ball.

Dribbling wasn't originally allowed in basketball.

In early games, players had to stay still when they caught the ball. The ball could only move by being passed to another player.

Basketball was invented in Massachusetts, U.S.A., in 1891 by a gym coach as an indoor winter sport.

Three-point shots weren't adopted by the National Basketball Association (NBA) until 1979.

The first slam dunk in college basketball, in 1944, was done by accident.

Basketball is the only major sport that originated in the United States.

The shortest NBA player ever was Tyrone Curtis "Muggsy" Bogues, who is 5 feet 3 inches (1.60 m) tall.

Wataru Misaka was the first person of Asian descent and the first person of color to play professional basketball in the United States. He was drafted by the New York Knicks in 1947.

The Shockers, Wichita State University's basketball team, have a mascot called WuShock, made all of wheat.

From 1967 to 1976, slam dunks were not allowed in college basketball.

The NBA was founded in 1946.

In the early 1900s, basketball courts were surrounded by a wire mesh fence.

The first basketball game was played in 1891.

Basketballs (and all types of balls) bounce higher when they are warm.

A flop is when a basketball player pretends to be hurt to make it look like a player on the other team fouled.

There are currently 30 teams in the NBA.

The oldest-running team in the NBA is the Sacramento Kings, which started in 1923.

Basketball is the seventh most popular sport in the world.

The first NBA game was in Toronto, Canada, in 1946.

Wheelchair basketball began after World War II as a way to help rehabilitate injured American war veterans. Women began playing in the mid-1960s.

In North Korea, if a player misses a free throw, their team loses a point.

In basketball, a steal is when the ball is taken from the other team.

Dr. James Naismith, the inventor of basketball, practices with his wife, Maude, in 1928.

The Cleveland Cavaliers once beat the Miami Heat by 68 points, the biggest gap for any victory.

In the 1970s, Lusia Harris was the first woman drafted by the NBA.

Basketball became an Olympic sport in the 1936 Summer Games in Berlin, Germany.

The average basketball hoop is **10 FEET (3 M) TALL**, the same height as a single-story building.

In 1962, Philadelphia Warriors player Wilt Chamberlain scored a record-breaking 100 points in one game against the New York Knicks.

The NBA logo was modeled after Los Angeles Lakers player Jerry West.

The Philadelphia 76ers were originally called the Syracuse Nationals. The team got a new name when it moved to Philadelphia in 1963.

Burnie, the Miami Heat mascot, has a basketball for a nose.

Basketball player Metta Sandiford-Artest got a record 73-game suspension for brawling with a spectator who threw a cup at him. At the time he was known as Metta World Peace.

More than 108,000 people packed into the stadium to watch the 2010 NBA All-Star Game, the largest crowd to ever watch a basketball game.

Jalen Lewis became a pro basketball player at only 16 years old.

In 1950, Earl Lloyd became the first Black NBA player.

The Oregon Ducks won the first National Collegiate Athletic Association (NCAA) men's basketball championship in 1939.

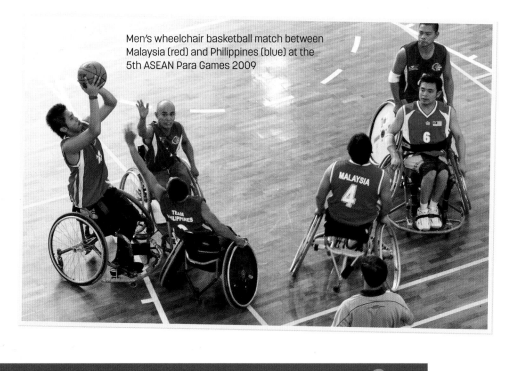

Men's wheelchair basketball match between Malaysia (red) and Philippines (blue) at the 5th ASEAN Para Games 2009

Professional basketball player **KAREEM ABDUL-JABBAR** scored a record-breaking 38,387 points in his career.

Diana Taurasi in action during a U.S.A. versus Latvia game

The longest winning streak for college basketball was the University of California, Los Angeles (UCLA), winning 88 games in a row from 1971 to 1974.

In wheelchair basketball, the hoop height is the same as standard basketball—10 feet (3 m).

A man once sunk a basketball into a hoop from 593 feet (181 m) above the ground. He threw the ball from the top of a dam in the Swiss Alps.

Wilt Chamberlain is in both the Basketball Hall of Fame and the Volleyball Hall of Fame.

Basketballs were originally brown, but they were changed to orange to be more visible for people playing and watching the game.

A standard basketball court is 94 feet (29 m) long.

The first basketball game in Europe was played in 1893 in Paris, France.

The NBA was called the Basketball Association of America (BAA) until 1949, when it merged with the National Basketball League.

The first Olympic basketball final took place on a repurposed tennis court during a rainstorm.

Basketball became a high school sport in the early 1900s.

The record for the most three-pointers shot in one minute is 31. That's nearly one every two seconds!

THE WNBA!

- The Women's National Basketball Association (WNBA) was founded in 1996.

- The Houston Comets won the first WNBA championship in 1997, and the next three after that.

- There are only 12 teams in the WNBA.

- The tallest WNBA player ever, Malgorzata Dydek, was 7 feet 2 inches (2.18 m) tall.

- WNBA player Diana Taurasi has scored more than 9,000 points in her career.

- WNBA basketballs are an inch (2.5 cm) smaller in circumference than NBA basketballs.

The United States won the gold medal in basketball at seven consecutive Olympics, from 1936 to 1968.

Women's basketball became an Olympic sport in 1976.

The bird in Twitter's logo is named Larry, after Boston Celtics basketball player Larry Bird.

The Philadelphia 76ers are named after the year 1776, when the Declaration of Independence was signed.

The longest successful backward shot sailed into the hoop from 82 feet 2 inches (25 m) away.

The International Basketball Federation (FIBA) is an organization that oversees all international basketball tournaments, including the Olympics.

In 1992, pro basketball players started competing in the Olympics.

The FIBA Basketball World Cup is an international tournament that happens every four years.

The United States and Yugoslavia have won more FIBA Basketball World Cups than any other country.

The biggest basketball stadium in the world is the Philippine Arena in Bulacan, Philippines. It's 106,800 square feet (9,922 sq m).

Rocket Rivers of the Harlem Globetrotters in a friendly game against the Washington Generals

The Harlem Globetrotters actually got their start in Chicago, not Harlem in New York City.

More than 30 countries have played in the FIBA Basketball World Cup games.

The Naismith Memorial Basketball Hall of Fame in Springfield, Massachusetts, U.S.A., was named after basketball's inventor James Naismith.

The longest NBA game lasted 78 minutes and had six overtimes.

In 1992, Sergei Belov from Russia became the first international player to be awarded a spot in the Basketball Hall of Fame.

A dog was once trained to bounce a soccer ball off its nose into a basketball hoop.

The world's longest shot was 112 feet 6 inches (34.3 m) and took place in 2014.

The first basketball hoop was made of a peach crate.

The Philadelphia 76ers had a record-breaking 28-game losing streak from 2014 to 2016.

Libyan basketball player Suleiman Ali Nashnush was 8 feet 0.5 inches (2.45 m) tall. He holds the record as the tallest basketball player.

Some people play basketball while riding unicycles.

NBA players can run up to 4 miles (6.5 km) in a single game.

Space Jam is the highest-earning basketball movie of all time. It brought in $90 million from theatergoers.

At 19 years old, Los Angeles Lakers player Kobe Bryant was the youngest player to ever start an NBA game.

The average NBA player can jump 28 inches (71 cm) in the air.

Off the court, LeBron James is left-handed. But he trained himself to be mainly right-handed on the court.

An American who's 7 feet (2.1 m) tall has a 17 percent chance of playing in the NBA.

The area of a basketball court just below the net is known as the "key."

MICHAEL JORDAN HAS OVER $1.5 BILLION, MAKING HIM THE WORLD'S RICHEST BASKETBALL PLAYER.

ORIGINALLY, EACH HALF OF A BASKETBALL GAME WAS JUST 15 MINUTES.

Turn to page 223 for the answers!

174 Totally Random Facts About

Super Science and Terrific Tech

Computers, Cars, and Other Cool Creations

Cutting Edge

75 Totally Random Facts About *ROBOTS* and *OTHER TECHNOLOGY*

Astronaut Steve Robinson is anchored to a robotic arm on the ISS during a space walk.

A robot is a machine that is designed to do tasks without human help. Most robots do not look like people.

Instead of using lawn mowers to cut the grass at their offices, Google rents 200 goats to chew the lawns.

When the first video camera recorder came out in 1956, it cost $50,000 and was the size of a piano.

THERE ARE THREE ROBOTIC ARMS ON THE INTERNATIONAL SPACE STATION (ISS).

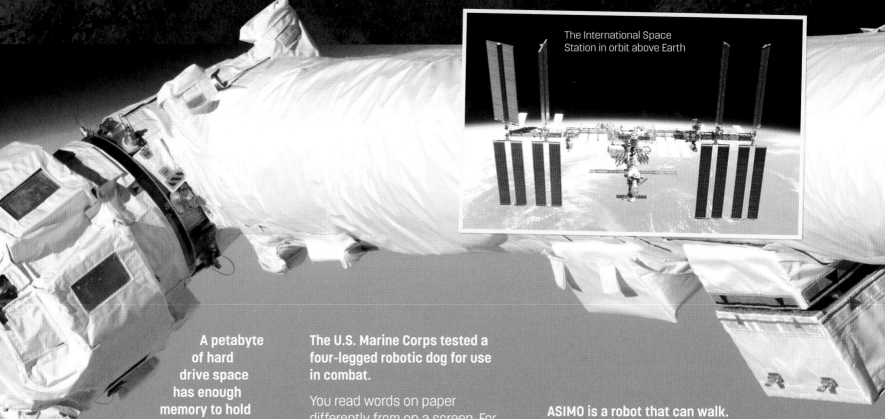

The International Space Station in orbit above Earth

A petabyte of hard drive space has enough memory to hold more than 13 years of HDTV shows.

Until 1995, registering a domain name was free. As of 2021, it costs about $200 for a two-year period.

The first digitally operated robot was invented in 1954.

The computer Alexa stores everything you ever tell it.

In 1826, the first photograph ever shot took 8 hours to expose. By 1839, it only took 15 minutes.

Famous video game character Mario was named after the landlord for Nintendo's warehouse.

A figure of Mario from the Nintendo Super Mario Bros. game series

The U.S. Marine Corps tested a four-legged robotic dog for use in combat.

You read words on paper differently from on a screen. For one thing, people blink less when reading from a computer.

Robots only do what humans program them to do.

GPS is free to use, but it costs several million dollars to operate each day.

The first computer mouse, invented in 1964, was made of wood.

In Antarctica, scientists tested an under-ice robot that could one day search for extraterrestrial life in space.

November 30 is Computer Security Day.

The SIAR project is a sewage inspection robot.

Around 85 percent of all sent emails are spam.

Spam mail was named after a brand of canned meat.

The first American alarm clock, invented at 1787, could only ring at 4 a.m.

In 2010, the U.S. Air Force used 1,760 PlayStation 3 consoles to build a supercomputer.

ASIMO is a robot that can walk.

The bar code was first used on a store product in 1974, on a pack of chewing gum.

The company name Yahoo came from a 1726 book called *Gulliver's Travels*; the Yahoos were a race of rude people.

In 2004, the @ symbol became the first new character added to Morse code in 60 years.

Amazon's first name was Cadabra.com, and it only sold books.

For more than 40 years, robots have been used to defuse bombs.

Picaboo was the original name for Snapchat.

The first autocorrect didn't use a dictionary. It used a program for commonly misspelled words.

Janken is a robot that "wins" the guessing game rock-paper-scissors 100 percent of the time. Its secret? It cheats.

The first email was sent in 1971.

On average, Google processes 3.5 billion searches a day.

Moxi is a robot with humanlike features that's designed to help nurses care for patients.

Nintendo was originally a playing card company.

"Phantom vibration syndrome" happens **when you sense your phone vibrating, but it isn't actually ringing.**

Some cell phones use Braille technology for blind people.

Japan is the robot capital of the world. More than 50 percent of all robots are made there.

Colossus, which was built between 1934 and 1945 by British code breakers, was the world's first digital computer.

It took Pokémon Go 19 days to reach 50 million users.

The first time a Nintendo Game Boy went to space was with a Soviet cosmonaut in 1993.

In 2017, a social robot in Saudi Arabia named Sophia was the first robot to be granted citizenship to a country.

The first four game controllers from Nintendo

The first personal computer sold exclusively for homes was the Apple II.

A gynoid is a female robot.

Robophobia is the fear of robots.

Modern-day smartphones have more computing power than the Apollo 11 module that landed on the moon in 1969.

Cell phones carry 10 times more bacteria than a toilet handle.

Robots can vacuum, cut grass, and do your laundry.

Lightbulbs were introduced to the public by Thomas Edison in 1879.

In 1945, ENIAC (Electronic Numerical Integrator and Computer) became the first computer built in the United States. It was as big as a ballroom.

The first cell phone sold in stores was the size of a brick and cost almost $4,000.

Like a real human body part, robotic body parts can read human brain signals and respond.

The first smartphone was the Simon Personal Communicator, which came out in 1994.

Bluetooth technology is named after Harald "Bluetooth" Gormsson, a king of Denmark and Norway during the 10th century.

Humans didn't invent electricity. It's a natural phenomenon.

Most robot voices are female.

The first cell phone call, placed in 1973, was made by the inventor to brag about his invention to his rival.

LED bulbs have a lifetime between 20,000 and 30,000 hours. That's 20 times longer than a traditional lightbulb.

Some factories rely on robots to do work that's not safe for people.

THAT'S SO RANDOM:

Robots Are Taking Over the World!

TODAY THERE ARE ABOUT 60 MILLION ROBOTS IN THE WORLD. BUT BY 2050, THERE MAY BE AS MANY AS 9.4 BILLION WORLDWIDE. That's more robots than humans! That's the prediction of a British futurologist, anyway. Dr. Ian Pearson doesn't have a crystal ball. But he is a scientist who studies the future. **He believes that robots will be commonplace in the majority of homes, doing chores like cooking and cleaning for families.** He also predicts that central heating in houses will be replaced by "smart heating" that will use infrared beams directed at your skin to personally adjust body temperature. **Dust will be vacuumed up by drones, and by 2075 clothing fabric will clean itself by shaking off dirt.** Although this all sounds too good to be true, Pearson did predict the use of text messages long before they existed—so he may be onto something!

A MICROSCOPIC MACHINE
CALLED A NANOROBOT
CAN BE USED TO HELP
SURGEONS DURING
OPERATIONS.

Robot farmers will soon help the agriculture industry by planting seeds, watering, and harvesting crops.

The first Apple logo featured Sir Isaac Newton sitting under an apple tree.

The bar code was invented in 1952; it was first used to label railroad cars.

Robots have been on Mars.

Recycling your cell phones can help save gorillas. Recycling reduces mining in gorilla and other wildlife habitats.

Cell phones contain gold.

A restaurant in China uses robot chefs.

An injured toucan in Brazil got a new beak made with a 3-D printer.

A robot named Raptor runs twice as fast as a human. It was inspired by the velociraptor, a dinosaur from the Cretaceous period that can run up to 29 miles an hour (46 kmh).

The world's fastest roller coaster, located in Abu Dhabi, United Arab Emirates, can travel 150 miles an hour (241 kmh).

In the future, cloning could help bring back extinct animals.

The first cat clone was a feline in Texas named CC, short for CopyCat, in 2001.

It took the internet seven years to reach 50 million users.

Androids are robots that look like people.

The first computer mouse got its name from the cord trailing the box, which looked like a mouse's tail.

THE AVERAGE AMERICAN DRIVES ABOUT 627,000 MILES (1,009,059 KM) IN THEIR LIFETIME, WHICH IS EQUAL TO 25 TRIPS AROUND THE WORLD.

Out for a Spin

99 Totally Random Facts About CARS

Smart car

A vintage French car advertisement

Cars were first designed in Europe in the late 1800s. • **The Ford Model T, nicknamed the Tin Lizzie, was America's first affordable car.** • The sounds you hear on the highway aren't coming from cars' engines. The noise you hear is the cars' tires coming in contact with the road at high speeds. • **The first picture on a license plate was a potato. It appeared in Idaho in 1928.** • A man from Sweden once got a speeding ticket for more than $1 million while in Switzerland. • **In 1985, a car engine was removed and replaced in 42 seconds. It usually takes 8 to 15 hours.** • Some car tires are made with walnut shells. • **The first speeding ticket was issued in 1896. The driver was going 8 miles an hour (13 kmh).** • The first "car" Henry Ford invented was called a quadricycle. • **Some race cars can be driven upside down in a tunnel going at 120 miles an hour (193 kmh).** • The fastest car on Earth—the SSC Tuatara— has a top speed of 282.9 miles an hour (455.3 kmh). • **The most miles ever driven by a single car is 3,000,000 (4,828,032 km).** • The

A Ford Model T

person who invented cruise control, which can keep a car driving at a constant speed, was blind. • **The average car has around 30,000 parts.** • In 163 countries, the steering wheel is on the left-hand side of the car. Drivers in 76 countries have their steering wheels on the right. • **The steering wheel was invented in Cleveland, Ohio, U.S.A., in the 1890s.** • The United States uses around 50 percent of the world's gasoline. • **The most popular car color is white.** • Before 1912, car tires were white. • **Some cars are powered by vegetable oil.** • After returning from the moon, astronaut Buzz Aldrin worked as a car salesman. • **In the 1200s, a monk predicted cars would one day exist. He said vehicles would no longer need animals to pull them, and they would move much faster.** • American actor John Wayne loved wearing his cowboy hat so much, he raised his car's roof so he could wear it while he drove. • **You can sleep in a bed made from a vintage car at a hotel in Germany.** • Driving slowly in traffic wastes up to 3 billion gallons

A Cadillac limo, the longest limousine in the world

(11.3 billion L) of gasoline each year. ● **The world's longest limousine is 100 feet (30.5 m) long and has 24 wheels.** ● In 1916, more than half the cars in the world were Ford Model T's. ● **About three out of every four drivers have had a flat tire.** ● A car needs at least half an ounce (15 ml) of gasoline to get started. ● **It's illegal to drive a car with a dirty license plate in Russia.** ● The first automobile race in the United States featured cars that could reach an average speed of 5 miles an hour (8 kmh). ● **Volvo means "I roll" in Latin.** ● A billion cars are currently being used across the globe. ● **Carmakers get new design ideas by studying how animals have adapted to nature.** ● The smallest car in the world is about 25 inches (64 cm) tall and less than 50 inches (127 cm) long. ● **In 2021, a flying car made a 35-minute test flight between two cities in Slovakia.** ● In 1900, about a third of cars were electric. ● **In Switzerland, it's illegal to slam a car door after 10 p.m.** ● The world's first gasoline-powered automobile was built in 1886 by a German inventor named Karl Benz. ● **NASCAR driver Richard Petty won a record 200 races during his career.** ● An air bag can fully inflate in 0.04 seconds. ● **Windshield wipers used to be hand-operated.** ● More than 50 percent of people sing while driving. ● **Before cars were invented, some science fiction writers thought people would ride**

in carriages that were pulled by electric-powered horses. ● The Long Island Motor Parkway in New York, built in 1908, was the first road made exclusively for cars. ● **Even before a car hits the road for the first time, gathering the materials—including steel, plastic, and rubber—to make the car creates harmful carbon dioxide emissions that cause air pollution.** ● The world's first roadway is now used only for bicycles. ● **The first limousine, made in 1902, didn't have windows or a door for the driver.** ● When stretch limos were invented in 1928, they were mainly used to take musicians and their instruments from one place to another. ● **The first type of car to have air conditioning was the limousine.** ● The U.S. president's limousine is nicknamed "The Beast." ● **The first smart car—a type of car made by a German company—was produced in 1994, but only sold in the United States in 2008.** ● The

NASCAR Driver Richard Petty

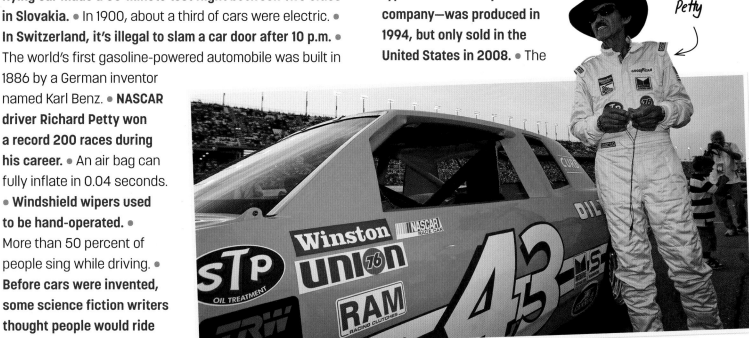

Mustang hubcap

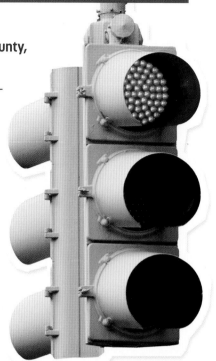

first fully functioning flying car had retractable wings. • **The first NASCAR race was held in 1948.** • The aerocar, the world's first-ever functioning flying car, was built in 1949 and had a wingspan of 34 feet (10 m). • **Shark fins have inspired some race car's designs.** • The oldest functioning car was made in 1884, using coal, paper, and wood for fuel. It still functions today! • **Some cars can communicate with other cars while on the road.** • Some cars have built-in massage chairs. • **Like some nocturnal creatures, cars with night vision can detect people or animals nearby.** • More than 85 percent of a car's parts can be recycled. • **A 1936 car called the Scarab looks like a giant beetle.** • A designer in France made a three-wheeled car commonly called the "electric egg." • **In 2010, 20 people set a world record for the most people to fit inside a smart car.** • Around 73 percent of cars in Brazil run using ethanol, which comes from sugarcane plants. • **In 1913, the Ford Model T became the first car to ever be built on an assembly line.** • In New York City, honking a car horn when it's not an emergency is illegal. • **Around 14 percent**

of the land in Los Angeles County, California, U.S.A., is used for parking. • In France, 14-year-olds are allowed to drive a small two-seater car called a VSP (car without a license). • **The average smart car is only 8.5 feet (2.6 m) long.** • The first sketch for the mini car was drawn on a napkin in the late 1950s. • **A group of 41 people can squeeze into a Toyota RAV4.** • A car is the safest place to be during a lightning storm. The car's metal blocks keep the electricity from entering the car. • **The first car with a radio was built in 1930.** • The average age of a car is

A Scarab minivan from 1936

around 12 years old. • **Highway hypnosis happens when a person drives for so long that they start getting sleepy.** • In the United States, 60 percent of carbon monoxide pollution is due to cars. • **Steel is the most common metal used to make cars.** • Steam-powered cars, driven until the 1900s in some countries, took around 30 minutes to start. • **Early cars were driven using a lever.** • Some car companies are working to develop self-driving cars. • **A car traveling 60 miles an hour (97 kmh) would take 165 days to reach the moon.** • People driving red cars get more speeding tickets. • **A man drove the same car for 82 years.** • The longest traffic jam spanned 109 miles (175 km) of roadways in France. • **Nevada was the first U.S. state to allow self-driving cars on the road.** • Between 1908 and 1927, more than 15 million Ford Model T cars were built. • **The best-selling car ever made is the Toyota Corolla.** • The car company Ferrari only makes 14 cars each day.

Ferrari

Cleaner Cars

• Countries—including Germany, Norway, and Costa Rica—are setting deadlines to stop the use of regular cars and get drivers to switch to eco-friendly hybrid and electric cars instead.

• **A driver can save 15 to 20 percent on fuel if they drive a hybrid car instead of a traditional model.**

• Hybrid electric cars recharge their batteries when the driver puts on the brakes, a process called regenerative braking.

• **Regenerative braking gathers kinetic energy from the wheel's motion so it's not wasted.**

• About half of the cars on Norway's roads are either electric or hybrid.

• **Electric cars are quieter than other cars on the road. Some countries require carmakers to add warning noises so people walking or cycling nearby can hear them.**

• As of 2021, nearly 2 million electric vehicles are in use in the United States.

• **Britain will ban the sale of gasoline- and diesel-powered cars starting in 2030.**

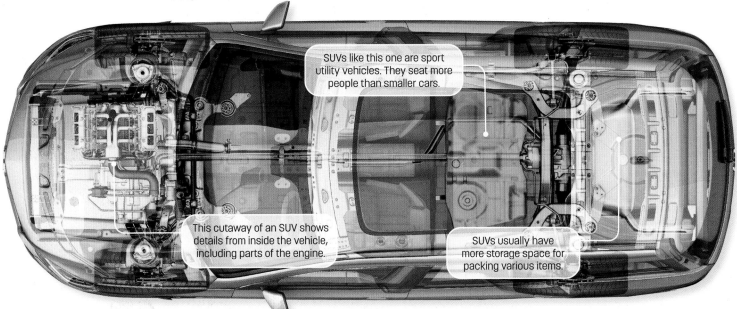

SUVs like this one are sport utility vehicles. They seat more people than smaller cars.

This cutaway of an SUV shows details from inside the vehicle, including parts of the engine.

SUVs usually have more storage space for packing various items.

EVERY MINUTE, 115 NEW CARS ARE BUILT AROUND THE WORLD.

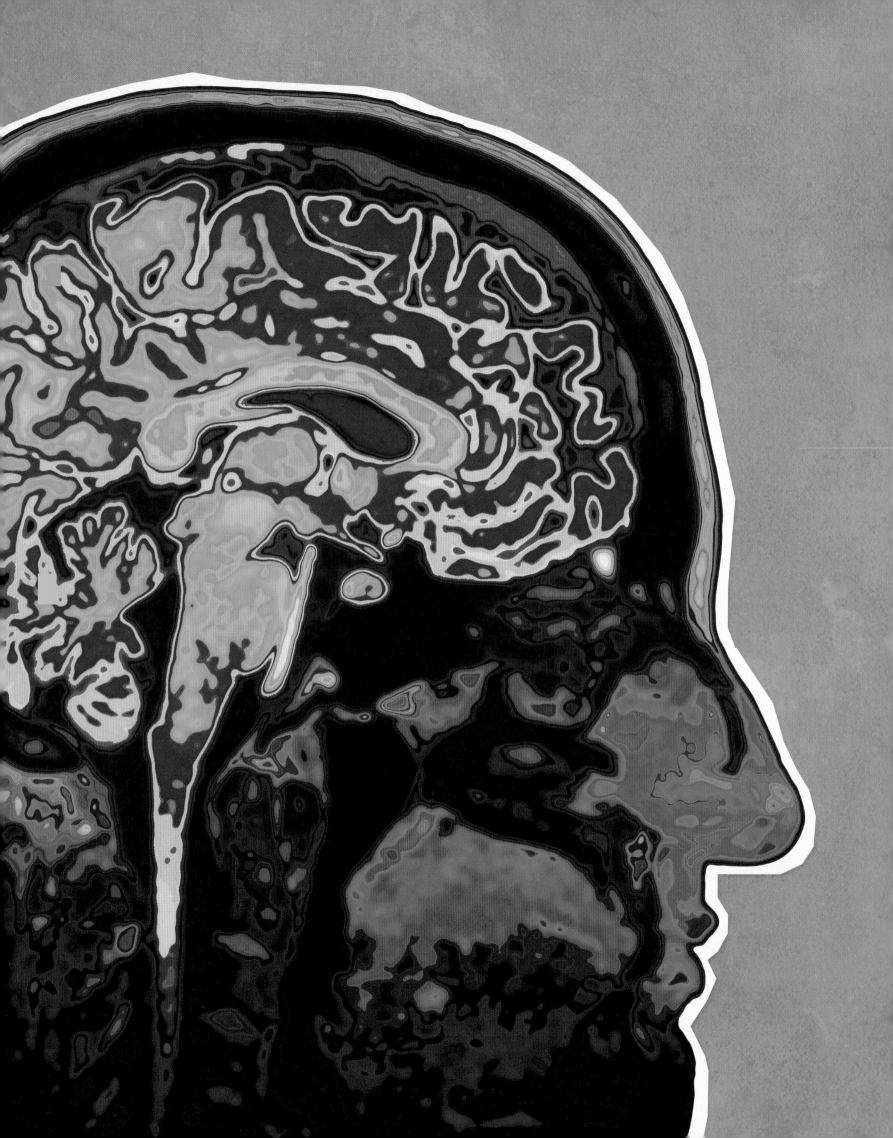

143 Totally Random Facts About

The Amazing Human Body

Bones, Belly Buttons, Brains, and Blood

HUMANS HAVE MORE
MUSCLES IN THEIR
FACES THAN ANY OTHER
MAMMAL ON EARTH—
MORE THAN 40 IN TOTAL.

From Head to Toe

THE ELEMENTS IN THE HUMAN BODY CAME FROM STARDUST.

/43 Totally Random Facts About the HUMAN BODY

Your body loses water as you breathe.

Nearly half of a person's body weight is in their muscles.

The jawbone is the human body's hardest bone.

The skeleton renews itself about every 10 years.

On average, people breathe in about 2,000 gallons (7,570 L) of air per day.

Fingers bend and move about 25 million times throughout a person's life.

The thickest part of the skin is on the soles of the feet and palms of the hands.

Your lungs have tiny hairs that can taste bitter flavors.

The brain uses 20 percent of the oxygen in your entire body.

Women's hearts beat faster than men's hearts.

The lungs of an adult male can hold about 1.6 gallons (6 L) of air.

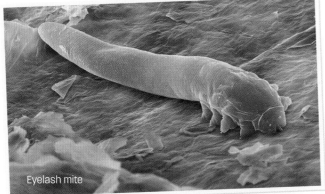
Eyelash mite

There are more than 200 joints in the human body. Joints are places where two bones meet, and they enable us to bend and move.

Caterpillars have more muscles than people do.

Your brain can be more active at night than during the day.

We all have tiny mites living on our faces.

Muscle produces energy three times faster than fat does.

About 1 out of every 200 people are born with an extra rib. It's more common in women than men.

Humans have goose bumps that make our hairs stand up so we look more threatening to predators.

About 25 percent of your bones are in your feet.

The longest bone in your body, the femur, is in your thigh.

Humans are the only animals that have chins.

The only bone not connected to a joint is the hyoid bone in the throat.

Bone marrow grows faster than any other tissue in the body.

The distance between your wrist and your elbow is about the same as the length of your foot.

The hip muscle, called the sartorius, is the body's longest muscle.

The shoulder blade is connected to the body with 17 different muscles.

Human teeth are as strong as shark teeth.

When you crack your knuckles, the sound you hear is bubbles bursting in the fluid around the joints.

The smallest muscle in the body, the stapedius in the middle ear, is only about 0.4 inches (10 mm) long. That's about half the width of a nickel.

Some of your taste buds die and regrow every two weeks.

You use 200 muscles when you take a single step.

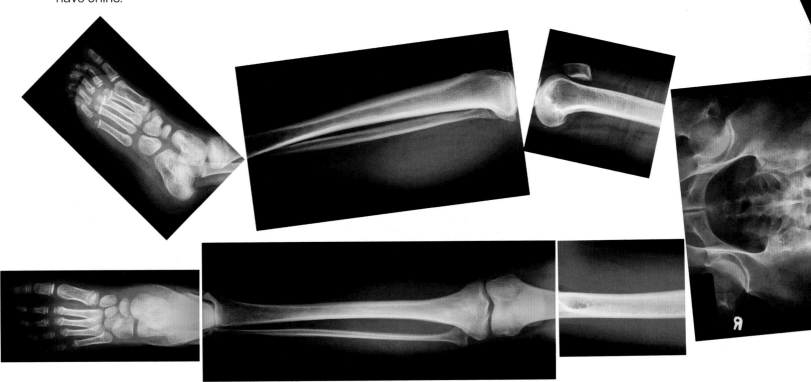

A HUMAN BEING IS MADE UP OF 7,000,000,000,000,000,000,000,000,000 (7 OCTILLION) ATOMS.

Every time you breathe, your ribs move. That's about 8 million times a year.

The nose can detect a trillion different scents.

Your lungs are the only organ that could float in water.

The average person will shed 93 pounds (42 kg) of skin in their lifetime.

The average kid's body has 60,000 miles (96,560 km) of blood vessels. Adults have 100,000 miles (160,930 km).

The brain only weighs about 3 pounds (1.4 kg).

An average person produces enough saliva in their lifetime to fill 182 bathtubs.

The word *muscle* comes from a Latin term meaning "little mouse."

Sweat is odorless until it mingles with the bacteria on your body.

Babies have more than 300 bones, but adults have only about 206—that's because some of the bones fuse together as we grow.

Everyone has a unique tongue print.

About 2,000 human cells can fit on the head of a pin.

The brain produces enough electricity to power a small lightbulb.

Your heart can beat faster or slower depending on the music you listen to.

You have more bacteria in your mouth than there are people in the world.

If uncoiled, the DNA in all the cells in your body would stretch 10 billion miles (16 billion km), enough to travel to and from the sun 61 times.

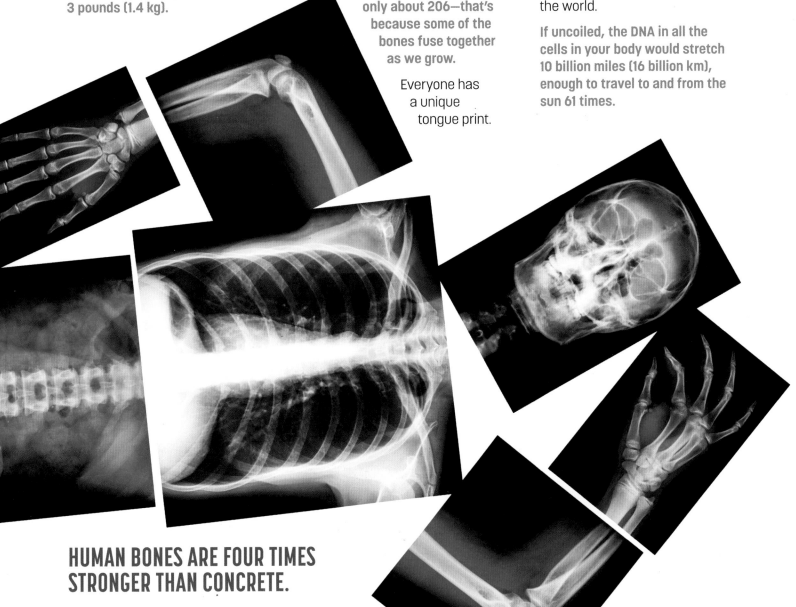

HUMAN BONES ARE FOUR TIMES STRONGER THAN CONCRETE.

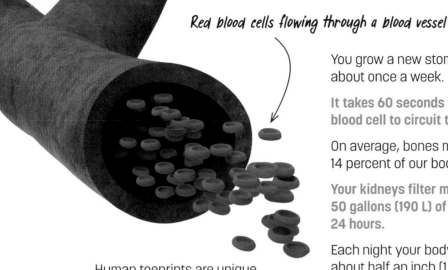

Red blood cells flowing through a blood vessel

You grow a new stomach lining about once a week.

It takes 60 seconds for a single blood cell to circuit the body.

On average, bones make up only 14 percent of our body weight.

Your kidneys filter more than 50 gallons (190 L) of fluid every 24 hours.

Each night your body lengthens about half an inch (1.25 cm), but you shrink back in the morning because of gravity.

Skin is the largest organ in the body.

Fingernails grow a tenth of an inch (0.25 cm) each month.

You can't swallow and breathe at the same time unless you're an infant.

The average person has around 100,000 hairs on their head.

The average person has around 5,000 taste buds.

Masseters, cheek muscles in your jaw, are some of the strongest muscles in the body.

It's impossible to tickle yourself.

Human bodies produce light, but not enough to be visible.

There are more than 60 species of bacteria living in your belly button.

A heart can beat more than 3 billion times in one lifetime.

Adults have about 32 teeth.

Humans are the only mammals that blush.

About 7 to 8 percent of a person's weight comes from the blood coursing through their veins.

Every day, the body sends oxygen through 1,000 miles (1,600 km) of airways.

Fingernails grow faster than toenails.

The human brain is wrinkly.

Human toeprints are unique like fingerprints.

The food you eat travels down a 30-foot (9 m) tube running from your mouth to your behind.

Your heart could pump enough blood during your lifetime to fill 1,800 train cars.

Brains keep developing for more than 40 years.

The human body has more than 600 muscles.

Teeth are the hardest substance in your body.

NERVE IMPULSES TRAVEL AS FAST AS 170 MILES AN HOUR (274 KMH) TO AND FROM THE BRAIN.

Brain

Spinal cord

Nerve

Human Water Balloon!

WHILE OUR BODIES MAY FEEL STURDY, WE ARE MORE LIQUID THAN SOLID. When babies are born, they are 78 percent water. By the time they turn one, that number drops to 60 percent. According to scientists, our lungs are 83 percent water, our muscles and kidneys are 79 percent water, and our brains and hearts are 73 percent water. **Our bodies depend on water for many reasons.** Water plumps up and gives structure to all of our cells. **In fact, it makes up 70 percent of each cell in the body.** It also acts as a natural buffer around our organs and the spinal cord. It greases our joints and makes saliva so we can talk without our lips sticking together. **Water also takes in nutrients so our bodies work properly, and it helps us remove waste.**

Belly buttons have special hairs that catch lint.

Your body makes about 2 cups (0.5 L) of sweat every day, and a lot more if you exercise.

The ancient Egyptians put honey on cuts to kill the germs. The stickiness also helped make the bandages stick.

Primates, including humans, are the only animals that have fingernails.

The stomach of an adult can hold half a gallon (1.9 L) of food.

The liver can grow back if part of it is removed.

You can survive without a gallbladder.

Blood is always red, but it is reddest when it has just left the heart and is full of oxygen.

Only about 21 percent of the air that you breathe is oxygen.

Strands of hair contain traces of gold.

Someone once spent $15,000 at an auction for a lock of Elvis Presley's hair.

Identical twins do not have identical fingerprints.

If you smoothed out the brain, it would be about the size of your pillow.

The brain's network of neurons looks like a spiderweb.

The muscles in a human's heart never take a break.

Thanks to the muscles in your forearms, your fingertips are so strong that they can support the weight of your entire body.

You blink more than 10 million times a year.

Humans are born with almost all the neurons they will ever use.

Some people can hear their eyeballs moving in their heads.

People who stay up late have more nightmares than people who go to bed early.

As you breathe in and out, most of the air goes through only one nostril. Every few hours, the air shifts to the other nostril. This is why, when you have a cold, it often seems like only one side of your nose is clogged at time.

Ancient Egyptians believed that the heart did all the thinking.

Your feet have 250,000 sweat glands. They can produce more than a pint of sweat each day.

The body can detect taste in 0.02 seconds.

Our bones are nearly one-third water.

About 60 percent of your brain is made of fat.

Your hair grows about 6 inches (15 cm) every year.

Every day, your nose produces about 1 cup (0.25 L) of mucus.

The tongue is made of eight different muscles.

Humans lose about 50 to 100 hairs each day.

EVERY CELL IN THE BODY DEPENDS ON THE HEART.

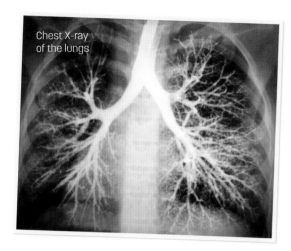

Chest X-ray of the lungs

All three bones in the human ear could fit together on top of a penny.

The muscles in the eyes are the body's fastest muscles.

Our eyes can see 10 million different colors.

Humans spend about a year of their lives going to the bathroom.

The left lung is a bit smaller than the right lung, to make room for the heart.

Earwax protects the inside of the ears by helping to trap dust and dirt before they can enter.

The capsule endoscopy camera is a tiny capsule-like camera that is swallowed so it can take pictures of the digestive tract.

About 95 percent of your skin is covered in hair.

YOUR BODY HAS ENOUGH BACTERIA TO FILL UP A SOUP CAN.

Every human has one of the four main blood types: A, B, AB, or O.

A handshake spreads 10 times as much bacteria as a fist bump.

Your brain can hold a million gigabytes of information—more than 3,000 times as much as a typical laptop computer.

To stay hydrated, doctors recommend drinking 8 cups (1.9 L) of water a day.

The heart pumps blood through its artery at a rate of 1 mile an hour (1.6 kmh).

Your body sweats to cool you down when you get too hot.

Water helps the body digest carbohydrates and proteins, which provide the body energy and materials for growth.

The human skull is made up of 22 different bones.

The jaw is the only bone in the skull that moves.

Over the course of your lifetime, you will replace your skin about 1,000 times.

Our bodies release toxins when we pee.

Earwax is not wax. It's a mixture of fat, skin cells, sweat, and dirt.

There are 37 trillion cells in your body.

The brain does not feel pain.

Babies hiccup in the womb.

The acids in your stomach are strong enough to etch metal.

Your nerves send messages to and from your brain through the spinal cord.

Though they are not bone, teeth are part of the skeletal system.

The digestive system converts food into nutrients that are used by the body's cell to make energy.

Humans spend about a third of their lives asleep.

The small intestine is longer than the large intestine.

Our eyeballs stay almost the same size for our entire lives.

One drop of blood holds 250 million red blood cells.

The muscular system

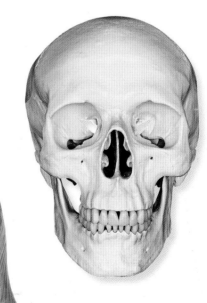

YOUR BRAIN CAN HOLD AS
MANY AS A QUADRILLION BITS OF
INFORMATION THROUGHOUT YOUR LIFE.

201 Totally Random Facts About

Stellar Space

Planets, Stars, and Galaxies

Far-Out!

147 Totally Random Facts About SPACE

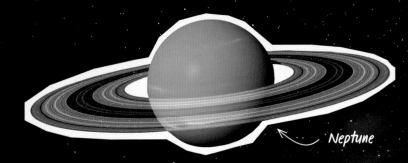

Neptune

There are eight plants and five known dwarf planets in our solar system. • **Stars don't actually twinkle. They look like they are twinkling because their light bounces through Earth's atmosphere.** • Jupiter spins faster than any other planet in our solar system. • **The largest group of canyons in our solar system is on Mars. The canyons stretch from about the same distance as Washington, D.C., to California.** • Uranus rotates backward, like Venus. • **Stars are gigantic balls of hydrogen and helium gas.** • Mars is one of the most explored bodies in our solar system. • **Mars has two moons: Phobos and Deimos.** • Scientists have counted more than 1 million asteroids so far. • **Stellar black holes are the most common type of black hole. They form from the collapse of a massive star.** • Eleven Earths could fit side by side inside the center of Jupiter. • **Though Neptune is farther from the sun, Uranus is the coldest planet in our solar system.** • Mercury is the smallest planet in our solar system. It is slightly larger than Earth's moon. • **Pluto has five moons.** • The sun is about 92 percent hydrogen and 8 percent helium. • **Our solar system has more than 200 known moons.** • Beneath its continents, Earth's crust is about 19 miles (31 km) deep. • **A nebula is a massive cloud of gas and dust particles floating in space.** • From Mercury's surface, the sun would appear about three times larger than it does from the surface of Earth. • **Total solar eclipses will disappear**

A **SPACE SUIT** weighs about 280 pounds (127 kg).

THE MILKY WAY is just one of about 100 billion galaxies in the universe.

in about 600 million years as the moon moves farther and farther away from Earth. • Scientists think Jupiter's core is solid and possibly about the size of Earth. • **A supernova is an explosion of a massive star.** • The pressure on Venus is so strong that if you were standing on its surface, it would feel like you were more than 2,640 feet (805 m) under the ocean. • **Saturn has 82 confirmed moons, more than any other planet in our solar system.** • Halley's comet passes by Earth every 75 years. The first recorded sighting of the comet was in 239 B.C., more than 2,000 years ago. • **A single season on Uranus lasts 21 years.** • A black hole is at the center of most galaxies. • **Mars and Earth have similar landforms.** • Proxima Centauri is the closest star to the sun. • In Roman mythology Jupiter is the god of the sky and king of the gods. • **Astronomers discovered a scorching-hot**

Stars Are Everywhere!

THERE ARE MORE STARS IN THE SKY THAN GRAINS OF SAND ON EARTH. How do we know? Researchers at the University of Hawaii **counted the grains of sand in a single teaspoon.** They then multiplied that number by the number of teaspoons it would take to scoop up all the sand in the deserts, beaches, and marshes around the world. Not surprisingly, they got to a gigantic number: **7 quintillion, 500 quadrillion grains.** Now just imagine there are 10 times more stars than that, which are visible from Earth through a telescope. Using a powerful telescope and a calculator, astronomers guestimate that, **at a minimum, there are 70 sextillion stars—that's a 7 followed by 21 zeros!** In the Milky Way alone, there are approximately 100 billion stars.

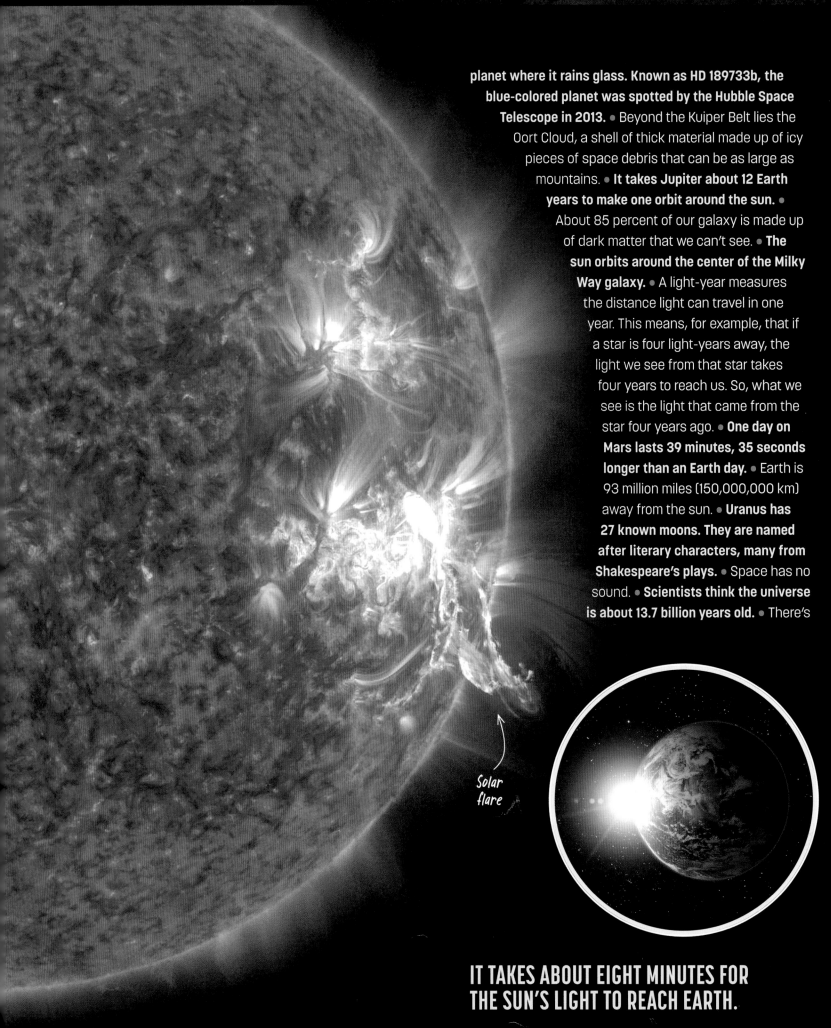

planet where it rains glass. Known as HD 189733b, the blue-colored planet was spotted by the Hubble Space Telescope in 2013. • Beyond the Kuiper Belt lies the Oort Cloud, a shell of thick material made up of icy pieces of space debris that can be as large as mountains. • **It takes Jupiter about 12 Earth years to make one orbit around the sun.** • About 85 percent of our galaxy is made up of dark matter that we can't see. • **The sun orbits around the center of the Milky Way galaxy.** • A light-year measures the distance light can travel in one year. This means, for example, that if a star is four light-years away, the light we see from that star takes four years to reach us. So, what we see is the light that came from the star four years ago. • **One day on Mars lasts 39 minutes, 35 seconds longer than an Earth day.** • Earth is 93 million miles (150,000,000 km) away from the sun. • **Uranus has 27 known moons. They are named after literary characters, many from Shakespeare's plays.** • Space has no sound. • **Scientists think the universe is about 13.7 billion years old.** • There's

Solar flare

IT TAKES ABOUT EIGHT MINUTES FOR THE SUN'S LIGHT TO REACH EARTH.

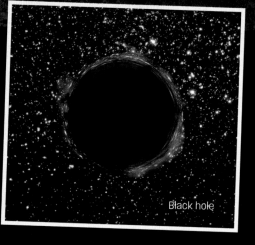
Black hole

a planet made of diamonds that is twice the size of Earth. ● **One day on Mercury is equal to about 178 Earth days.** ● Nine Earths could fit side by side in the center of Saturn. ●

Billions of years ago Mars was a warmer and wetter planet with a thicker atmosphere. ● The sun has a far-reaching magnetic field that moves through the solar system by solar wind. ● **Galaxies are categorized by their shape. There are three main groups: spiral galaxies, elliptical galaxies, and irregular galaxies.** ● The International Space Station makes 16 orbits around Earth every 24 hours. ● **Neptune was discovered in 1846.** ● Scientists believe that there was once water on Venus. ● **Earth is not a perfect sphere. It is flattened at its top and bottom and bulges at its center.** ● Uranus was discovered in 1781. ● **Though Mercury is closer to the sun, Venus is the hottest planet in our solar system.** ● There are thousands of other known planets, called exoplanets, orbiting their own stars in the Milky Way. ● **The sun's core is a scorching 27 million °F (15 million °C).**

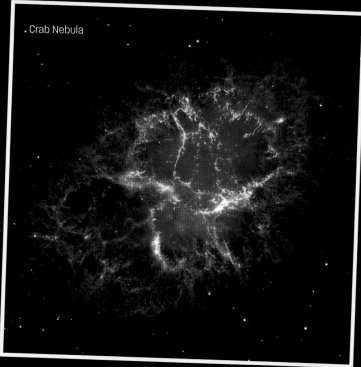
. Crab Nebula

The Hale-Bopp comet

● Most asteroids are pieces of minor planets from our solar system. ● **The surface of the sun is hot enough to make diamonds melt.** ● The longest space walk by astronauts took almost nine hours. ● **Uranus is the only planet that rotates on its side.** ● The sun is the only star in our solar system. All the other stars we see are much farther away. ● **The Milky Way is a spiral-shaped galaxy.** ● The sun

IT TAKES SATURN 29 EARTH YEARS TO MAKE ONE ORBIT AROUND THE SUN.

Image from Cassini spacecraft in Saturn's shadow looking back toward the sun

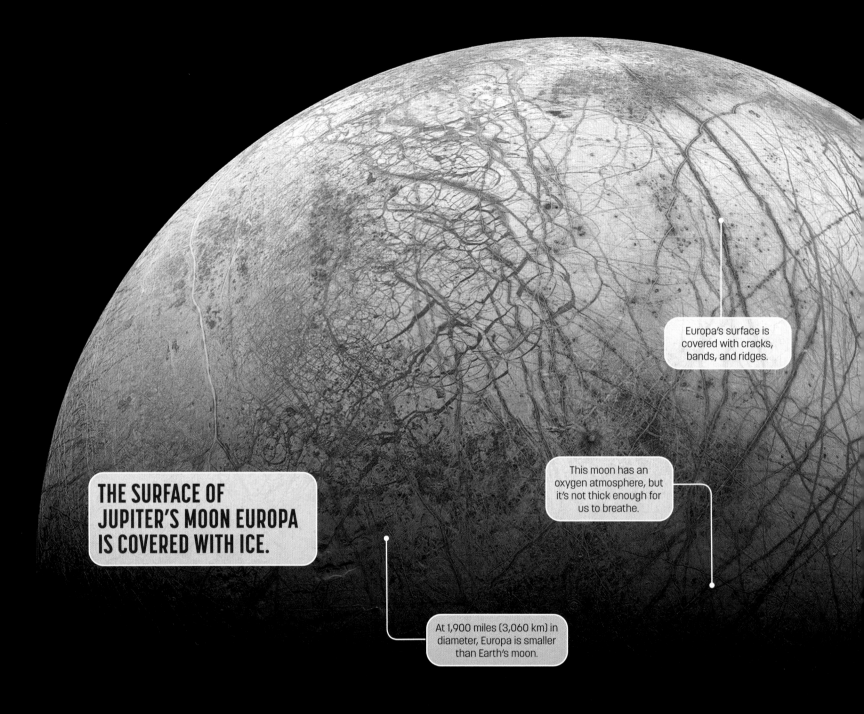

Europa's surface is covered with cracks, bands, and ridges.

This moon has an oxygen atmosphere, but it's not thick enough for us to breathe.

THE SURFACE OF JUPITER'S MOON EUROPA IS COVERED WITH ICE.

At 1,900 miles (3,060 km) in diameter, Europa is smaller than Earth's moon.

has dark spots. These areas are cooler than the rest of its surface. ● **Asteroids and comets contain water.** ● Scientists believe Jupiter's moon Ganymede has a large saltwater ocean under its icy surface. This ocean might contain more water than all of Earth's oceans. ● **Jupiter's other moons, Callisto and Europa, along with Saturn's moon Enceladus might have saltwater oceans under thick ice, too.** ● One day on Neptune is about 16 hours long. ● **A day is longer than a year on Venus.** ● Solar flares are explosions that happen on the sun's surface. ● **If all of the known asteroids were clumped together, their mass would make up less than 10 percent of the mass of the moon.** ● Neptune has at least

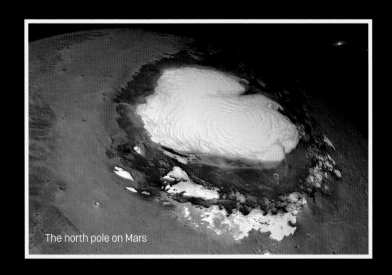

The north pole on Mars

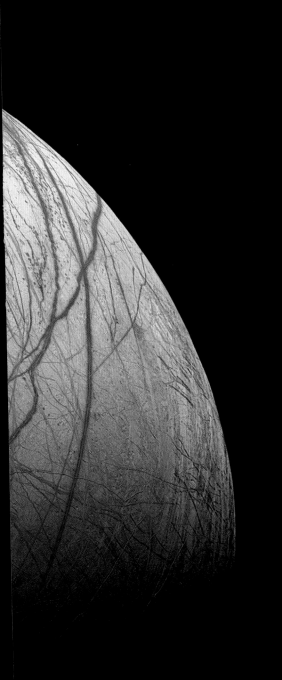

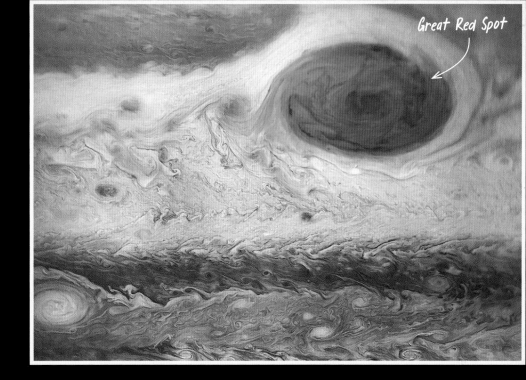

Great Red Spot

THE GREAT RED SPOT IS A STORM ON JUPITER THAT HAS BEEN RAGING FOR HUNDREDS OF YEARS.

Pluto

five main rings. • **Out past the planets in our solar system lies the Kuiper Belt. This ring of icy bodies is home to the dwarf planet Pluto.** • New stars are formed in nebulae, earning nebulae the nickname "star nurseries." • **Mercury, Venus, Mars, Jupiter, and Saturn are visible from Earth without a telescope. Uranus and Neptune are too far to see with the naked eye.** • Venus and Mercury are the only two planets without moons. • **Phobos and Deimos, Mars's moons, were discovered just six nights apart.** • A day on Saturn only lasts about 11 hours. • **There are more trees on Earth than stars in the Milky Way galaxy.** • Ceres was first discovered in 1801. Now considered a dwarf planet, it is the largest object in the asteroid belt. • **The sun is a star.** • The largest known star in the universe is named UY Scuti. It has a radius that is about 1,700 times larger than the radius of the sun. • **Within our galaxy, only around two or three known supernovas occur every 100 years.** • Jupiter's moon Ganymede is the largest moon is our solar system. • **The oldest rocks known on Earth are about 4.2 billion years old.**

Mars

Deimos

Phobos

NASA astronaut and SpaceX Crew-3 Commander Raja Chari during a training session, 2021

Thousands of people apply to be NASA astronauts each year, but only **8 TO 14 ARE CHOSEN.**

• Only about 5 percent of the universe is visible.• **Uranus gets its greenish-blue color from the methane gas in its atmosphere.** • "Spaghettification" is a phenomenon that happens when a star comes too close to a black hole and is stretched out like spaghetti from the intense pull of gravity. • **More than 1 million Earths could fit inside the sun.** • Sirius, the brightest star in the night sky, is 8.6 light-years away, which means the light we see is from 8.6 years ago. • **Venus has constant hurricane-force winds that blow high in the planet's atmosphere.** • Saturn's rings are made of ice, rock, and dust. • **Jupiter has rings. They are very faint, so we can't see them as clearly as the rings of Saturn or Uranus.** • Neptune has 14 known moons. • **Earth has a**

magnetic field that helps keep out the sun's solar wind. • Our solar system is 26,000 light-years from the center of the Milky Way, too far away for us to actually see what it looks like. • **Stars can be red, orange, yellow, white, or blue.** • Mars is known as the red planet because iron minerals in the soil rust, causing the soil to look red. • **The sun is the largest object in our solar system, making up about 99 percent of the solar system's mass.** • Venus is named for the Roman goddess of love. • **Neptune is the windiest planet in our solar system. Winds can reach speeds of more than 1,200 miles an hour (1,930 kmh).** • The word *Earth* comes from a German word and means "the ground." • **Uranus has 13 known rings. The inner rings are dark, and the outer rings are colorful.** • Red stars are the coolest; blue stars are the hottest. • **The sun is almost a perfect sphere.** • Mercury and Venus are the only planets in our solar system without moons. • **The size of the particles that make up Saturn's rings range from about the size of a grain of sand to roughly the size of a house.** • It takes Mercury 88 days to make one orbit around the sun. • **Most of Earth's fresh water is found in ice caps and glaciers, and in the ground.** • The Andromeda galaxy will one day collide with our Milky Way galaxy. • **One day on Uranus is about 17 hours long.** • The first mission to Mars took place in 1965. • **Scientists think an Earth-size object might have hit Uranus long ago and knocked over the planet.** • Venus has a thick, toxic atmosphere that traps in the sun's heat. • **Our solar system formed 4.5 billion years ago from a dense cloud of**

Because **MARS HAS LESS GRAVITY THAN EARTH,** a person weighing 110 pounds (50 kg) on Earth would weigh 42 pounds (19 kg) on Mars.

interstellar gas and dust. • Jupiter has 79 known moons, and even more that have not yet been confirmed by scientists. • **Sunsets on Mars look blue.** • A quasar is an incredibly bright distant object that gets its energy from a black hole. One recently discovered quasar gives off light that is the equivalent of about 600 trillion suns. • **Uranus was the first planet found using a telescope.** • Earth is the only planet known to have liquid water on its surface. • **Saturn has seven main rings. They are each made up of many smaller rings.** • Our solar system is located in one of the spiral arms of the Milky Way. • **Mercury's surface is covered with craters, like Earth's moon.** • The surface of Venus is hot enough to melt lead. • **It takes four hours for the sun's light to reach Neptune. Because Neptune is so far away, it remains mostly dark.** • The sun's gravity keeps everything in our solar system in orbit around the sun. • **Earth is the only planet in our solar system not named after a Greek or Roman god or goddess.** • Uranus is named after Ouranos, the Greek god representing heaven. It is the only planet named after a Greek god. • **The Canis Major dwarf galaxy is the closest known galaxy to the Milky Way.**

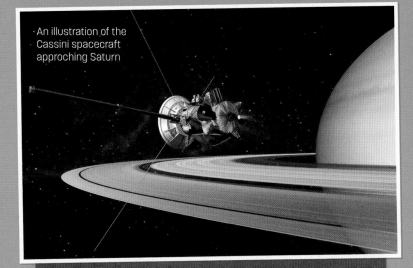

An illustration of the Cassini spacecraft approaching Saturn

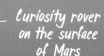

Curiosity rover on the surface of Mars

An illustration of astronauts on Mars

Exploring the Unknown

- Sojourner, the first rover to explore the surface of Mars, landed on the planet in 1997.

- **Mars is the only planet where we've sent rovers to explore the surface.**

- In 1962, NASA sent Mariner 2 to fly by Venus, making Venus the first planet to be explored by spacecraft.

- **NASA has sent nine spacecraft to visit Jupiter.**

- More than 40 spacecraft have explored Venus.

- **The Cassini spacecraft spent 13 years exploring Saturn. When its mission was over, it was purposely flown into Saturn's atmosphere, where it vaporized.**

- The Cassini spacecraft spent a total of 20 years exploring space.

- **The European Space Agency's spacecraft Huygens landed on Saturn's moon Titan in 2005.**

- Only one spacecraft has flown by Neptune. Voyager 2 reached the planet in August 1989, and sent back the first close-up images of the planet.

Night Light

54 Totally Random Facts About the MOON

ON EARTH, WE ALWAYS SEE THE SAME SIDE OF THE MOON—THE NEAR SIDE

A full harvest moon rises in Scituate, MA, on September 16, 2016.

THE MOON FORMED WHEN A MARS-SIZE ROCK NAMED THEIA SMASHED INTO EARTH. THE SMASHED BITS CREATED THE MOON.

The moon is Earth's closest neighbor in space.

The moon formed about 4.4 to 4.5 billion years ago.

Only 12 people have walked on the moon.

The moon's glow comes from the sun shining on it.

The moon's dark patches are basins that were once filled with lava.

Moon rocks have been brought back to Earth.

The moon orbits Earth in an oval-shaped path known as an ellipse.

Just like Earth has earthquakes, the moon has moonquakes.

There is no wind on the moon.

The moon is almost perfectly round.

Some moonquakes are caused by Earth's ocean tides.

The moon's innermost core is solid, just like Earth's inner core.

There are mountains on the moon's surface.

Earth's moon is bigger than Pluto.

The moon is the second densest satellite, after Jupiter's moon Io.

The moon's diameter is about 25 percent the diameter of Earth.

It takes 29.5 days for the moon to orbit once around Earth.

More than 400 tree seeds went up to space on the Apollo 14 mission to the moon in 1971. The seeds were brought back to Earth and planted. They are now known as "moon trees."

When the moon's orbit is closest to Earth, it makes ocean tides higher.

The moon is slowing down Earth's rotation by 1.5 milliseconds each century.

Earth's moon is the fifth largest moon in our solar system.

The moon's surface is dark.

The sun is almost 400 times bigger than the moon.

Earth is 400 times closer to the moon than it is to the sun.

Moon rock

The moon is a dusty ball of rock.

Moonquakes are much weaker than earthquakes but can last much longer—up to 30 minutes.

There is frozen water in the soil of the moon.

Buzz Aldrin salutes the American flag

A United States flag was planted on the moon in 1969 by astronauts Neil Armstrong and Buzz Aldrin.

About 49 moons could fit inside Earth.

Most of the moon's craters came from asteroids that hit more than a billion years ago.

Eratosthenes crater
Copernicus crater

WE ONLY EVER SEE 60 PERCENT OF THE MOON'S SURFACE FROM EARTH.

We see the same side of the moon all the time, but the amount of it that's in sunlight changes.

The temperature on the moon can go from a scorching 260°F (127°C) when the sun hits its surface to a frigid minus 280°F (−173°C) at night.

You would weigh much less on the moon because the moon's gravity is much weaker.

Basalt is a type of rock found on both Earth and the moon.

Many ancient societies used the moon to track time.

A lunar eclipse is when Earth blocks the sun's rays from hitting the moon.

A solar eclipse is when the moon blocks the sun's rays from hitting a part of, or a path over, Earth.

Oysters close during a full moon.

The moon has no atmosphere, so there is no weather.

Doodlebugs dig larger holes during a full moon.

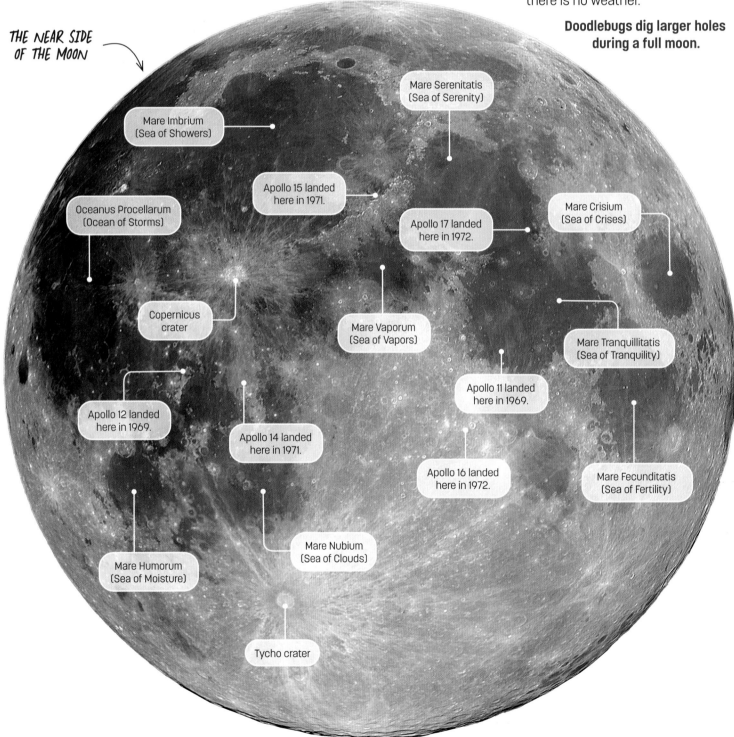

THE NEAR SIDE OF THE MOON

Mare Imbrium (Sea of Showers)

Mare Serenitatis (Sea of Serenity)

Apollo 15 landed here in 1971.

Oceanus Procellarum (Ocean of Storms)

Apollo 17 landed here in 1972.

Mare Crisium (Sea of Crises)

Copernicus crater

Mare Vaporum (Sea of Vapors)

Mare Tranquillitatis (Sea of Tranquility)

Apollo 12 landed here in 1969.

Apollo 11 landed here in 1969.

Apollo 14 landed here in 1971.

Apollo 16 landed here in 1972.

Mare Fecunditatis (Sea of Fertility)

Mare Nubium (Sea of Clouds)

Mare Humorum (Sea of Moisture)

Tycho crater

A beach at low tide

Earth's ocean tides are caused by the gravity of the moon and the sun.

Scorpions have a special protein that causes them to glow blue in the moonlight.

Once a year after a full moon, hundreds of species of corals spawn at the same time in the Great Barrier Reef.

Scientists think that water got to the moon by comets and asteroids that crashed into it long ago.

Some nocturnal animals use moonlight to navigate during night.

THE MOON IS SLOWLY MOVING AWAY FROM EARTH.

A photograph of Earth and the moon's surface as seen from Apollo 8 as it was in lunar orbit. The photograph, taken by astronaut William Alison Anders, is called "Earthrise."

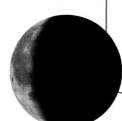

GOING THROUGH A PHASE

- **The phases of the moon are determined by how much of the side facing Earth is lit by the sun.**

- **The moon has eight phases: new moon, waxing crescent, first quarter, waxing gibbous, full moon, waning gibbous, third quarter, and waning crescent.**

- **A new moon is seen when the moon is between Earth and the sun and the lighted side of the moon faces away from Earth.**

- **A crescent moon, a curved thin sliver of reflected sunlight, is what we see from Earth when our planet blocks the sun's rays from much of the moon.**

- **A full moon happens when we see it opposite from the sun, so it's all completely lit up.**

Random Roundup

Neat Numbers, Sweet Celebrations, Fun Foods, and Other Totally Cool Topics

Singular Digits

48 Totally Random Facts About NUMBERS

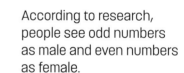

One day has 86,400 seconds in it.

Two and five are the only prime numbers that end with either a 2 or 5.

Roman numerals were first invented between 700 and 900 B.C. to trade goods.

A 50-dollar bill circulates for about 12 years.

Pick a number and multiply it by three, then add the digits together. That total can always be divided by three.

More people pick seven as their favorite number than any other number.

BEES CAN COUNT TO FOUR.

According to research, people see odd numbers as male and even numbers as female.

The temperature minus 40 is the same in both Fahrenheit and Celsius.

Tetraphobia is a fear of the number four.

Two is the only even prime number.

The opposite sides of dice always add up to seven.

196

CATS ARE SAID TO HAVE NINE LIVES BECAUSE THE NUMBER WAS SPECIAL TO MANY CULTURES.

Lucky 7

HALAL
IDCP

CARNE NORTE

Serving Suggestion

In China, the number four is considered unlucky because the word for it sounds similar to the word for death.

The four-second rule says that cars should stay at least four seconds behind the car in front of them.

The angles of every type of triangle always add up to 180 degrees.

Seven is believed to be a lucky number.

You could arrange the 52 cards in a single deck in more ways than there are atoms on Earth.

The numerical system was based on the Hindu Arabic numeral system created more than 1,000 years ago.

Thirteen is believed to be an unlucky number.

In Thailand, 555 is used in text messages to say "hahaha" because five is pronounced "ha."

Most months have 31 days.

Four is the only number spelled with the same number of letters as the number it represents.

Dragonflies have about 30,000 lenses in each eye. Humans only have one lens in each eye.

Italians used to fear Friday the 17th. That's because the Roman numeral for 17—XVII—can be rearranged to create the Latin word for "my life is over."

The word *hundred* comes from the Old Norse word *hundrath*, which actually means "120."

The record for counting fastest to one million is 89 days.

In a room of 70 people, there's a 99.9 percent chance two people will have the same birthday.

Numerology is the study of how significant numbers impact a person's life.

Many hotels and office buildings in Europe and the United States do not have a 13th floor or a room numbered 13.

The fear of the number 13 is called triskaidekaphobia.

There's a man from California who can solve questions as fast as a calculator can.

The first name for the game Sudoku was Latin Squares.

If an internet page takes longer than three seconds to load, nearly half of all people won't wait to read it.

MAPS NEED ONLY HAVE FOUR COLORS TO ENSURE THAT NO COUNTRIES THAT TOUCH HAVE THE SAME COLOR.

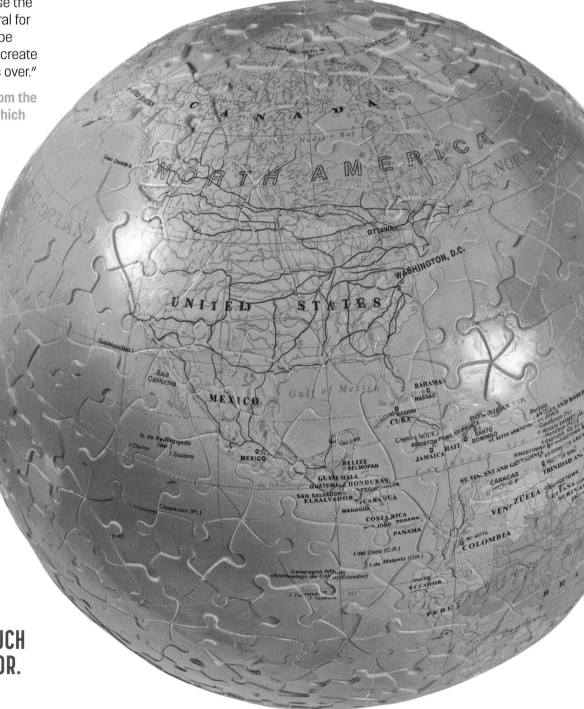

A dollar bill can be double-folded 4,000 times before it will tear.

It's a myth that it's impossible to fold paper more than nine times.

The number pi, which starts with 3.14, is celebrated on Pi Day each March 14.

You can arrange a Rubik's Cube in 43 quintillion different ways.

Denver, Colorado, U.S.A., has an elevation of 5,280 feet (1,609 m), which makes it exactly 1 mile (1.6 km) high.

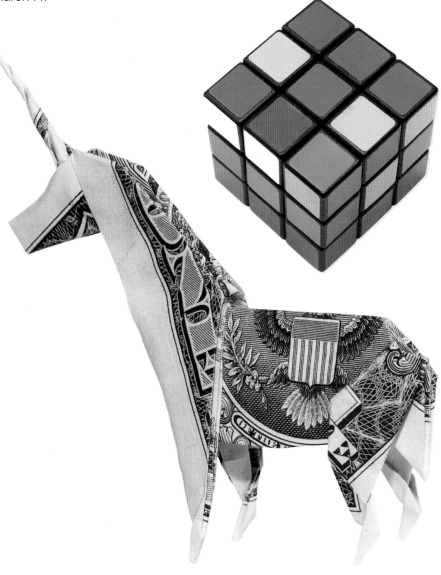

DENVER
CITY LIMIT
ELEV 5280 FT

THE NUMBER "O"

- **Dolphins and bees understand the concept of zero.**

- **Zero is the only number that can't be written in Roman numerals.**

- **The number 0 was invented at different times by multiple cultures.**

- **Because an even number is any number that can be divided by two and still be even, zero counts as an even number.**

- **The ancient Greeks didn't consider zero a number.**

- **A googol is a 1 followed by 100 zeros.**

- **A googolplex is a 1 followed by googol zeros. If you were to write it out in a book, the book would weigh more than the planet.**

- **In tennis, the score love means zero.**

Celebrate!

52 Totally Random Facts About HOLIDAYS AROUND THE WORLD

The tradition of decorating a Christmas tree started in Germany.

Kwanzaa was a holiday created by Dr. Maulana Karenga in 1966.

Potato pancakes called latkes are a traditional food eaten during Hanukkah.

The Chinese New Year, also called the Lunar New Year, doesn't have a set date because it follows the phases of the moon.

During Diwali, Hindu people light lamps to honor Lakshmi, the goddess of prosperity.

If you add up all of the gifts in "The Twelve Days of Christmas" song, you get 364.

Passover celebrates the Hebrews' freedom from slavery in ancient Egypt.

Though the United States celebrates Independence Day on July 4 (the date Congress approved the Declaration of Independence in 1776), freedom from England was officially declared two days earlier.

to celebrate the heritage and values of African American culture.

Hanukkah is an eight-day Jewish celebration of the Jews' victory over their enemies, which allowed them to keep practicing their religion.

In Japan, the emperor's birthday is a national holiday.

The dreidel, a traditional Hanukkah toy, is a spinning four-sided top.

Hanukkah is also called the Festival of Lights or the Feast of Dedication.

Some countries light fireworks to celebrate Christmas.

Cinco de Mayo takes place each year on May 5. On this day, people in parts of Mexico and the United States celebrate Mexico's victory over France in a battle that took place in 1862.

On January 6, families in Italy celebrate La Befana, a witch that leaves children presents.

Seven is a common number in Kwanzaa celebrations. It's the number of letters in the holiday's name and the number of days it lasts.

Both Chanukah and Hanukkah are correct spellings of the Jewish Festival of Lights. In fact, there are more than 20 different ways to spell it.

The letters on a dreidel represent a Hebrew phrase about Israel: "A great miracle happened there."

A dreidel

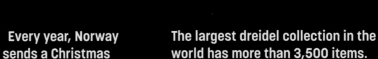

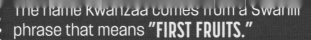
The name Kwanzaa comes from a Swahili phrase that means **"FIRST FRUITS."**

Every year, Norway sends a Christmas tree to Great Britain to thank the country for its help during World War II.

In Japan, May 5 is Kodomo no hi, also known as Children's Day. Japanese people honor their children and fly streamers to bring them good fortune.

In Ukraine, people decorate their Christmas trees with spiderwebs to bring good luck in the new year.

At Christmastime in Wales, people go caroling dressed as horses.

The first state to recognize Christmas as a holiday was Alabama.

In Mexico, people celebrate Día de los Muertos (Day of the Dead) to honor friends and family who have passed away.

A skeleton decorated for Día de los Muertos (Day of the Dead)

The largest dreidel collection in the world has more than 3,500 items.

The largest-ever gathering of people wearing holiday-themed sweaters was 3,473 people.

Random Roundup

On the Chinese New Year, dumplings are eaten as a symbol of prosperity.

The first known New Year's celebration was 4,000 years ago in ancient Babylon.

Muslims take part in a month of fasting called Ramadan. It ends with Eid al-Fitr, a food-filled festival with families sharing gifts and prayers.

Real Christmas trees are better for the environment than artificial ones.

In the Hindu religion, Diwali honors the gods and marks the beginning of a new year.

In Mexico, people carve radishes into works of art to celebrate Christmas.

Saint Patrick was a real person.

Saint Patrick

Hands covered in colorful powder during Holi

People throw colorful powder called *gulal* during Holi, or the Festival of Colors, to mark the end of winter in northern India.

During the fall, people from Nepal gather to celebrate the Hindu holiday of Dashain, which commemorates the victory of good over evil.

To celebrate Hanukkah, Jewish people light a candle in a menorah for eight nights, recite prayers, and sing songs.

Songkran, a festival marking the Thai New Year, includes a giant friendly water fight.

On December 8, people of the Buddhist faith celebrate Bodhi Day, the day Prince Siddhartha Gautama became the Buddha.

To stop the theft of Christmas trees on campus, one university sprayed them with skunk scent.

The only bread allowed during Passover is matzo—a flat, cracker-like bread made without yeast.

Apples were the first Christmas tree decorations.

Hawaii commemorates Lei Day each May 1, celebrating the state's arts and culture.

People in Caracas, Venezuela, **ROLLER-SKATE** to church on Christmas.

A dragon at a Chinese New Year festival in Thailand

Turkey Day!

- "Jingle Bells" was originally written as a Thanksgiving song.

- **For every Thanksgiving since 1989, the U.S. president has pardoned a turkey. Two of those turkeys got a trip to a Disney theme park.**

- The first Macy's Thanksgiving Day Parade in New York City didn't include any balloons.

- **Americans eat roughly 46 million turkeys for Thanksgiving each year.**

- In 1941, President Roosevelt declared the fourth Thursday in November to be a national holiday: Thanksgiving.

- **The average person consumes 3,000 calories at a Thanksgiving dinner, the same amount found in 14 frosted donuts.**

- The first National Football League games played on Thanksgiving were in 1920.

THE AVERAGE AMERICAN PERSON EATS NEARLY 1 TON (900 KG) OF FOOD A YEAR.

Let's Eat!

107 Totally Random Facts About FOOD

lettuce being grown on the International Space Station

Grapes explode into fireballs when you microwave them.

For more than 200 years, people believed that tomatoes were poisonous.

Ice cream–like treats were first eaten 3,000 years ago in China.

Dark chocolate, in small amounts, is good for your health. Doctors believe it lowers the risk of certain diseases.

Most carrots were originally white or pale yellow. Early domestic carrots were purple and yellow.

The ghost pepper is 400 times hotter than Tabasco sauce.

Coffee beans aren't actually beans. They are seeds, or pits, from inside the coffee fruit.

The Chinese invented noodles more than 4,000 years ago.

You can only taste food if it's mixed with your saliva.

The longest pizza delivery on record was 12,346.6 miles (19,999 km), from Spain to New Zealand.

The first soft drink consumed in space was Coca-Cola. Pepsi was the second.

Bananas are technically a fruit and an herb. They're related to ginger.

There are more than 1,000 kinds of bananas grown worldwide. Each kind has a name, including Mona Lisa, Goldfinger, and Ice Cream.

If kept in the freezer, chocolate can stay fresh for six to eight months past its expiration date.

A single strand of spaghetti is called a spaghetto.

Peppers have more vitamin C than oranges.

About three-fourths of all the food eaten around the world is from only 5 animals and 12 plants.

Three grains—wheat, rice, and corn—make up more than half the calories people get from eating plants.

China is the world's largest producer of garlic.

Red and blue LED bulbs are used to encourage plant growth.

Astronauts have grown lettuce and kale in space.

Fruit salad trees in Australia grow six kinds of fruit.

Crackers have holes to prevent them from cracking as they bake.

Milk is white because of the protein in it.

Ketchup used to be sold as a medicine.

American cheese was invented in Switzerland.

Chickens can produce one egg a day.

Specially trained dogs and pigs are used to sniff out truffles, a rare and expensive kind of mushroom used in gourmet food.

A truffle

The food you eat affects your brain and your mood.

Applesauce was the first food eaten by the first American in space. The first person in space, who was a Soviet cosmonaut, ate beef and liver paste followed by chocolate sauce, both squeezed out of tubes.

Dynamite can be made using peanuts.

Onions release a gas that makes you cry when you cut them.

The largest potato ever grown weighed 11 pounds (5 kg), more than a newborn baby.

Candy canes were invented 350 years ago.

Arachibutyrophobia is the fear of peanut butter getting stuck to the roof of your mouth.

Honey never spoils.

French fries originated in Belgium, not France.

The ingredients on food packages are listed in order by weight.

The first pizzas sold in New York cost five cents.

Cuy, fried or roasted guinea pig, is a popular dish in Peru.

Ripe cranberries bounce.

An 11-year-old boy named Frank invented the Popsicle by accident in 1905.

The FDA, a U.S. government agency that oversees food safety, allows a certain number of bugs in food.

The difference between jelly and jam? Jam is made with fruit and jelly is made with fruit juice.

Fortune cookies were invented in San Francisco, not China.

Music can alter your sense of taste. High-pitched tunes can make foods taste sweeter, while low-frequency hums can make foods taste more bitter.

HAWAIIAN PIZZA was invented in Canada.

It takes a pineapple more than a year to grow.

The first frozen pizzas were sold in the 1950s. And in 1964 one of the earliest frozen pizza companies was run by a family named Pizza.

California is the world's fifth largest food supplier.

A potato is 80 percent water.

Your brain uses up **ONE-FIFTH** of all the energy from the food you eat.

Up to 40 percent of fresh fruits and veggies get tossed because they're thought to be too ugly to sell.

It's impossible to fry an egg on a hot sidewalk.

Wintergreen Life Savers mints sparkle in your mouth when you crunch them.

The biggest candy cane in the world was 51 feet (15.5 m) long.

The ancient Egyptians made marshmallows.

In Mexico, fried grasshoppers are sold in markets as a crunchy snack.

In China and Thailand, insects such as crickets and ants are slathered in chocolate and eaten.

In southern Africa, caterpillars are a regular part of some people's diet.

About 25 percent of the world's yearly hazelnut supply winds up in Nutella.

Chocolate dates all the way back to 900 B.C.

Cotton candy was invented by a dentist.

Cheese is not made of mold, but mold is added to some cheeses—like blue cheese—to enhance its flavor.

Nearly 2 billion candy canes are sold in the four weeks before Hanukkah and Christmas.

Ears of corn almost always have an even number of rows.

White chocolate doesn't actually contain any real chocolate.

In its original recipe, pound cake had exactly 1 pound (453 g) of every ingredient.

Froot Loops come in many colors, but they all taste the same.

No one knows for sure how Hershey's Kisses got their name.

Eating lots of carrots can turn your skin orange.

The average strawberry has 200 seeds.

Blueberry juice boosts memory in older adults.

Apples contain so much air, they can float in water.

It takes 26 minutes of walking to burn off the calories from one soft drink.

Eating more fish can reduce headaches.

Peppercorns, candy, cacao beans, and cheese have all been used as currency.

A sculptor once made an Abraham Lincoln statue out of a 1,000-pound (453-kg) block of cheese.

Americans chow down on nearly 50 billion burgers each year.

The chicken nugget was invented in the 1950s. It was originally called the Chicken Crispie.

Rotten eggs float, while fresh eggs sink.

The top of a pineapple can be cut off and replanted to grow a new one.

The largest chicken nugget of all time weighed a whopping 51.1 pounds (23.2 kg). It was 3.25 feet (1 m) long and 2 feet (0.6 m) wide.

The Aztecs believed that chocolate was a gift from the god of wisdom, Quetzalcoatl.

cacao pod

cacao beans inside pulp | cacao beans

COOL BEANS: CHOCOLATE'S MAGIC INGREDIENT

- **Cacao beans were so valuable that the Maya civilization used chocolate as money.**

- **About 70 percent of cacao comes from West Africa.**

- **The scientific name for the tree that produces cacao beans means "food of the gods."**

- **It takes 400 cacao beans to make 1 pound (454 g) of chocolate.**

Fried tarantula

People in Cambodia eat fried tarantulas as a fancy treat.

Worldwide, people drink more milk from goats than cows.

Despite its name, a peanut is not a nut. It's a legume, like a bean or pea.

Hot dogs, also known as frankfurters, were originally from Frankfurt, Germany.

A man named Joey Chestnut ate 76 hot dogs in 10 minutes, breaking his own world record of 75 hot dogs in 10 minutes.

Apples can last for a year in cold storage.

Corn is related to grass.

The average fast-food customer swallows 100,000 hairs from employees each year.

Some red food coloring is made from boiled bugs.

Cherries are related to roses.

Gold-wrapped sushi has been served in the Philippines.

Watermelons can be grown in cube and pyramid shapes.

A company in London created glow-in-the-dark ice cream.

You can plant an avocado pit to grow a new tree.

Native Americans use corn husks to make dolls.

The world's largest meatball contained more than 1,700 pounds (771 kg) of meat.

Every year people in Olney, England, race carrying pancakes in frying pans.

About 6.5 pounds (3 kg) of greenhouse gases are released to produce just one quarter-pounder burger.

THAT'S SO RANDOM:

The Power of Eating Plants!

BOTANISTS—SCIENTISTS WHO STUDY PLANTS—LOOK AT HOW FOODS GROW. If a food grows from a plant's flower and has seeds, it's a fruit. What if it grows from other parts of the plant, like the root, stem, bulb, or leaves, and it doesn't have any seeds? Then it's a vegetable! Since cucumbers grow from flowers and they have seeds, botanists label it a fruit. That means peppers, pumpkins, and tomatoes are all fruits, too, while lettuce, carrots, and potatoes are vegetables. No matter how you categorize them, **fruits and vegetables are an important part of our daily diet.** They're packed with vitamins and minerals that are essential to your well-being. They work hard to keep your body healthy and strong. They help shore up bones, heal wounds, and bolster your immune system. They also convert food into energy to **help you think, move, and run.** Fruits and vegetables are low in calories and fat, which means you can eat more to stay full without negatively affecting your health. They are naturally low in saturated fat and salt, and veggies and many fruits are low in sugar, too. They also have plenty of fiber to fill you up and boost the health of your gut. Many vegetables and fruits even contain phytochemicals, compounds that **can help protect against some diseases.** Pass the fruit and veggie platter, please!

PEOPLE CHUCK MORE THAN 100 TONS (90,720 KG) OF TOMATOES AT EACH OTHER DURING LA TOMATINA, AN ANNUAL FESTIVAL IN SPAIN.

Sticky Business

35 Totally Random Facts About CHEWING GUM

Gum is one of the oldest candies in the world. It dates back to the Stone Age.

The ancient Greeks chewed gum made from resin of the mastic tree.

Chicle, from sapodilla trees that grow in the rain forest, was one of the first main ingredients for gum.

There are more than 1,000 varieties of gum sold in the United States.

Bubble gum is pink because it's the only color the inventor had available to try.

The most popular flavors for gum are peppermint, spearmint, and cinnamon.

Michael Jordan regularly chewed gum during basketball practice to help him concentrate.

Bubble gum was invented in 1906 and was originally called Blibber-Blubber.

In 1888, gum was first sold in vending machines, in New York City subway stations.

THE SECRET TO BLOWING A BIG BUBBLE IS TAKING SLOW, DEEP BREATHS.

Bubblegum Alley in San Luis Obispo, California

San Luis Obispo, California, U.S.A., is home to the 65-foot (20-m)-long Bubblegum Alley, where the walls are covered in chewed gum. It has been there since the 1950s.

Some chimps chew gum.

About 100,000 tons (90,718 metric t) of bubble gum are chewed every year around the world. That's roughly the weight of 50,000 hippos!

It's a myth that bubble gum will stick to your intestines. However, if you swallow gum, the body can't digest it, so it's passed in one piece.

About 374 billion pieces of gum are sold per year around the world.

Singapore banned chewing gum in 1992. Officials took action after gum had ended up clogging the doors of subway trains.

Studies have shown that gum chewing can help with concentration and memory.

Chewing gum burns about 10 calories an hour.

DURING THE TWO WORLD WARS, AMERICAN SOLDIERS RECEIVED REGULAR GUM RATIONS.

Saliva flow increases about 10 times when you chew gum.

The first bubble gum cards sold in packs came out in the 1930s. The cards featured war scenes, Wild West cowboys, and athletes.

In most countries, chewing gum is not required to have an expiration date.

Gum stays rubbery no matter how long you chew it because the rubber base doesn't dissolve in water.

Archaeologists discovered what may be 5,700-year-old chewing gum—tar from a birch tree. It gave archaeologists clues about a woman who lived in the Stone Age.

What a Record!

- The largest bubble gum bubble blown was 20 in (51 cm) in diameter, a record set by a man in Alabama in April 2004.

- **In September 2014, a Guinness World Record was set for the most bubble gum bubbles blown in one minute: 15 bubbles!**

- The longest gum wrapper chain ever made was created by a retired teacher. The chain was nearly 20.2 miles (32.5 km) long.

- **The Guinness World Record for the largest bubble gum bubble ever blown with the nose was 11 inches (28 cm) in diameter.**

- The country with the record for the most gum producers is Turkey, with more than 60 manufacturers.

Chewing gum while taking a test can boost performance up to 40 percent.

September 30 and February 15 are both National Chewing Gum Day.

Chewing gum on an airplane can help prevent your ears from popping because the extra swallowing relieves air pressure.

Peanut butter can remove gum if it gets stuck in your hair.

According to a study done with high school students, chewing gum helps reduce stress by tricking the brain into think it's being fed.

Sugar-free gum prevents cavities by producing saliva, which can wash away plaque and bacteria.

Trick or Treat!

55 Totally Random Facts About *HALLOWEEN*

Some pumpkins can grow a whopping 60 pounds (27 kg) in a single day, which is about the weight of a six-year-old human.

Pumpkins float in water.

The U.S. government has a plan for surviving a zombie apocalypse, but it's considered a training exercise.

Halloween comes from a 2,000-year-old Celtic celebration called Samhain.

Shoppers spend $4.6 billion on candy during the two weeks leading up to Halloween.

The Irish introduced Halloween to the United States in the 1800s.

Illinois is the top-producing state for pumpkins.

The most popular Halloween costumes for kids are princesses and superheroes.

The most popular costume for dogs is a pumpkin.

The oldest official Halloween celebration, which included a parade and a bonfire, was in Minnesota in 1920.

More than 80 percent of parents admit to sneaking into their kids' Halloween candy.

Pumpkins have about 500 seeds.

According to legend, the White House is haunted by Abraham Lincoln.

Orange-and-purple Halloween crabs climb trees at night.

The largest pumpkin grew to be 2,624 pounds (1,190 kg).

Teraphobia is the fear of monsters.

The largest pumpkin pie was as long as a two-story building is tall.

The most popular Halloween candy in the United States is Skittles.

The largest jack-o'-lantern ever carved weighed as much as a horse!

The world record for apple bobbing was 37 apples in one minute.

October 30 is National Candy Corn Day.

Candy corn, invented in the 1880s, used to be called Chicken Feed.

You can buy specially themed candy corn for Christmas, Valentine's Day, and Easter.

Pumpkins are fruits.

During World War II, Tootsie Rolls were given to American soldiers to keep up their energy.

Austrians leave snacks out for dead relatives on Halloween night.

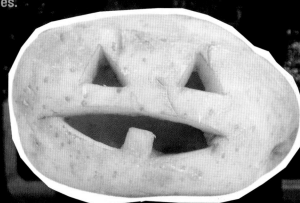

THE FIRST JACK-O'-LANTERNS WERE MADE OUT OF TURNIPS AND POTATOES.

There are more Halloween emojis than U.S. states.

"Pumpkin" comes from the Greek word *pepon*, which means "large melon."

The gargoyles on cathedrals are supposed to guard against evil spirits.

The largest pumpkin ever grown in the United States came from New Hampshire.

Scuba divers carve pumpkins underwater for a festival in Florida.

In western Canada, children say "Halloween apples" instead of "trick or treat."

There is a traditional Irish bread for Halloween called "brack," which is sweet and has raisins and a small toy inside.

Pumpkins were once considered a remedy for snakebites and freckles.

In Sweden, children dress up as ghouls and witches to trick-or-treat the Thursday before Easter.

Pumpkins come in many colors, including orange, red, green, yellow, white, tan, and even blue.

Fear of the dark is called nyctophobia.

Americans spend about $86.27 per family on Halloween every year.

"Monster Mash," a song about a mad scientist, was a number one hit in 1962.

Divers carve a halloween pumpkin underwater.

WARNING
ZOMBIE INFESTATION
THIS AREA UNDER STRICT
QUARANTINE
USE OF DEADLY FORCE IN EFFECT

During medieval times, witches were not pictured with pointy hats. Historians aren't quite sure where those came from.

THE NEXT FULL MOON ON HALLOWEEN WON'T OCCUR UNTIL 2039.

A dwarf planet called "The Goblin" was discovered on the outer reaches of our solar system beyond Pluto.

Anyone over the age of 16 in Bathurst, Canada, faces up to a $200 fine for trick-or-treating.

The record for the most jack-o'-lanterns on display goes to Keene, New Hampshire, with 30,581 glowing pumpkins around town.

The fear of Halloween is called Samhainophobia.

Eighty percent of Americans say that they can't imagine Halloween without candy.

The world record for the fastest pumpkin carving is 16.47 seconds.

There's a 7-foot (2-m)-long gummy python snake. It weighs 27 pounds (12 kg).

Black Cat Appreciation Day is August 17.

SPOOKY NATURE

- **The vampire squid gets its name from its red color and the tissue that connects its arms, making the squid look like it's wearing a cape.**

- **Zombie fungi release a chemical toxin to control the brain of their host, the ant.**

- **Ghost-faced bats like to roost in abandoned mines, tunnels, buildings, and caves.**

- **Skeleton shrimp have a very fitting name. These tiny, see-through creatures have strong claws to capture prey, and some can even change colors.**

- **A snake known as the death adder lies in wait before it strikes its unsuspecting prey with toxic venom. Once the prey dies, the snake digs in.**

Index

Ferris Wheel Day is **FEBRUARY 14TH.**

The first Ferris wheel was
BUILT IN 1893 and cost $385,000.

HOT AIR BALLOONS can't fly in the rain or on a windy day.

Photo Credits

Credits

Text and cover design copyright © 2022
by Penguin Random House LLC

All rights reserved. Published in the United States by Bright Matter Books, an imprint of Random House Children's Books, a division of Penguin Random House LLC, New York.

Bright Matter Books and the colophon are registered trademarks of Penguin Random House LLC.

Visit us on the Web! **rhcbooks.com**

Educators and librarians, for a variety of teaching tools, visit us at **RHTeachersLibrarians.com**

Library of Congress Cataloging-in-Publication Data is available upon request.

ISBN 978-0-593-45053-6 (trade)
ISBN 978-0-593-45054-3 (lib. bdg.)
ISBN 978-0-593-51620-1 (ebook)

COVER PHOTO CREDITS:
Front Cover Photos: Shutterstock (all)
Back Cover Photos: Dreamstime (center left); NASA (top right); Shutterstock (center right)

MANUFACTURED IN ITALY
10 9 8 7 6 5 4 3 2 1
First Edition

Produced by Fun Factory Press, LLC, in association with Potomac Global Media, LLC.

The publisher would like to thank the following people for their contributions to this book:
Melina Gerosa Bellows, President, Fun Factory Press, and Series Creator and Author; Priyanka Lamichhane, Editor and Project Manager; Rose Davidson, Editor; Jane Sunderland, Copy Editor; Chad Tomlinson, Art Director; Mary Stephanos and Steve Hoffman, Fact-checkers; Jack Pecau, Editorial Intern; Potomac Global Media: Kevin Mulroy, Publisher; Barbara Brownell Grogan, Editor in Chief, Thomas Keenes, Designer; Susannah Jayes and Ellen Dupont, Picture Researchers; Heather McElwain, Proofreader

BRIGHT MATTER BOOKS

TOTALLY RANDOM KIDS

SPOT THE 13 RANDOM DIFFERENCES:

p93 Awesome Animals

p157 Splendid Sports

p217 Random Roundup

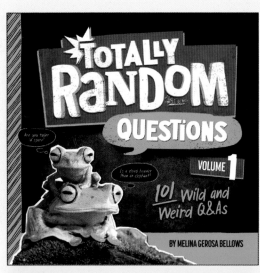

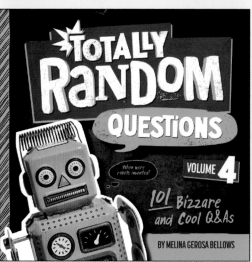